Surviving the naked truth about my father

## VENKE FEHLIS

with Malcolm J. Nicholl

Wuppertal Press • Santa Barbara, CA

VENKE by Venke Fehlis

Copyright © 2021 by Venke Fehlis

Published by
Wuppertal Press
66 Barranca Avenue
Santa Barbara, CA 93109
wuppertalpress@gmail.com

All rights reserved. No part of this book may be reproduced or transmitted in any form or by any means, electronic or mechanical, including photocopying, recording, or by any storage or retrieval system, except in the case of brief quotations embedded in critical articles and reviews, without prior written permission by the publisher.

Library of Congress Control Number: 2021902904

Publisher's Cataloging-In-Publication Data
(Prepared by The Donohue Group, Inc.)

Names: Fehlis, Venke, author. | Nicholl, Malcolm J., author.
Title: Venke : surviving the naked truth about my father / Venke Fehlis,
    with Malcolm J. Nicholl.
Description: Santa Barbara, CA : Wuppertal Press, [2021]
Identifiers: ISBN 9781736622308 (print) | ISBN 9781736622315 (ebook)
Subjects: LCSH: Fehlis, Venke--Family. | Germany. Geheime Staatspolizei--
    Officials and employees. | Illegitimate children--Norway--Biography. |
    Norway--History--German occupation, 1940-1945. | Norway--Biography. |
    LCGFT: Autobiographies.
Classification: LCC DL529.F44 A3 2021 (print) | LCC DL529.F44 (ebook) |
    DDC 948.104092--dc23

Copyeditor: Isabella Piestrzynska
Book and cover design: Illumination Graphics
Book production coordinated by To Press & Beyond,
www.topressandbeyond.com

Images courtesy of www.depositphotos.com
and wikipedia commons:
Bundesarchiv, Bild 183-A0706-0018-030 / CC-BY-SA 3.0, CC BY-SA 3.0
and Bundesarchiv, Bild 183-2008-0513-501 / CC-BY-SA 3.0, CC BY-SA 3.0

Printed in the United States of America.

# Dedication

For my son, Joe.
Without him, there would be no book.
There might even be no life.
At the beginning of this journey, he understood
where his mother needed to go.
His love, strength, and support have always been there.

# Prologue

Oslo, Norway. May 9, 1945.

*I*n the light of a spring evening, a young smartly dressed woman emerged from the door of her home in an upmarket neighborhood of Oslo, the Norwegian capital. In Europe, World War II had come to a bloody and messy end. As the blond, twenty-something woman gracefully stepped toward a highly polished black limousine, a uniformed chauffeur half-bowed and opened the passenger door, allowing her to disappear inside.

On her heels followed a man almost twice her age wearing a gray, starched military uniform and peaked cap. At least six feet tall, he nevertheless maintained a stiff, erect posture, disciplined by years of military life. A saber scar, a badge of honor, was clearly visible on his left cheek. He had all the bearings of a high-ranking officer, someone used to his commands being obeyed.

## Venke

Cradled gently in the officer's arms was a tiny bundle, a baby girl, just a little over three months old. The officer paused at the top of the steps and stared deeply at the innocent face of the child. He carefully studied each tiny feature as if committing it to memory, perhaps wondering if he would ever see that face again.

Walking past the chauffeur, who'd resumed his attentive sentry-like position at the passenger door, the officer tenderly handed the infant to the woman in the back seat in a strangely formal yet intimate manner.

Bending deep into the car he slowly lifted his head, reluctantly transferring his gaze from the baby to the woman and, in a muffled voice, strangled with emotion, told her, "If the worst happens, please know that in my last minutes I will think of you and only you. Remember that, only you."

The woman was my mother. That baby was me. I didn't know any of this until I was an adult and had embarked on a journey to discover the true circumstances of my early years. It was a quest born out of a hunger for the truth, a desire to discover my real identity as I struggled with many issues—a dysfunctional relationship with my disparaging, narcissistic, and alcoholic mother; living for too many years with a verbally and physically abusive husband; and fights with my own demons when I began to enjoy wine too much.

After being fed snippets of information over the years from my mother—a mélange of distortions, half-truths and outright lies—I began layer by layer to unravel the complex story that had been hidden from me. The ultimate shocking discovery: my father was Heinrich Fehlis, a high-ranking Nazi, the feared chief of Gestapo in Norway, and my mother, Else Johanne Schaug, was his young Norwegian mistress.

One of my father's last acts before killing himself rather than be captured by the Allies was to secretly negotiate for my mother and me to be smuggled into the safety of Sweden in return for the release of thousands of prisoners.

Part of the story was locked away in classified government files, sealed and marked not to be opened for twenty-four years, and part of the story was known to members of my family, who never talked about it. Some elements I uncovered by tracking down a friend of my mother's, as well as my half-brother in Germany and other Fehlis family members, who embraced me as one of their own and demonstrated more love to me than my own mother ever had.

While my story revolves around my search for my identity, there is no escaping the impact of the contentious relationship with both my mother and my husband and my personal battle to overcome my cravings for alcohol. It has been a long and painful journey. I have uncovered facts that many might feel were better never to have been discovered. I have unearthed the truth, the naked truth about my father. And I have survived and I am the better for it.

# Chapter One

"My daddy was a general."

I was about seven years old and bragged to a girl I'd just met that my father had been a general in the war. A German general. I thought it was something to be proud of and couldn't resist boasting about it. My mother and I lived with Mamma and Pappa—that's what I called my mother's parents—in their tiny apartment at Tøyengata 32, between the botanical garden and Grønland, a gritty, blue-collar neighborhood on Oslo's east side.

Home was two rooms and a kitchen on the top floor of a three-story walk-up, which, like many centuries-old European buildings, had no elevator. The apartment was a little cramped as we not only shared it with my grandparents but also my mother's two younger sisters. Three of us slept huddled together in a pull-out sofa bed in the living room. The other room doubled as a

## Venke

dining room and bedroom for my grandparents, who had to spend their nights in a pull-down Murphy bed. There was no hot water and we had a coal-burning stove. What was weird was that the kitchen was separated from the living room by a public corridor, mostly used by the three families that lived on that floor. We'd go from one room to the next, locking doors behind us so no one could steal anything. All the residents of the building shared two small bathrooms, both in the attic, one floor higher.

I was delighted to have made a new friend in the street outside our apartment building and hurried home, skipping up the stairs, eager to tell my mother. As soon as I walked into the room and saw anger blazoned across her face I was scared. I knew I had done something bad. Really bad. But what? My new friend's father had phoned my mother to tell her what I had said about my father and exactly what he thought of her. And he forbade his daughter from seeing me again.

"Venke," my mother warned me, "don't ever tell anyone again about your father."

She was so furious her entire body was shaking, and, as young as I was, I also sensed she was terrified. What was going on? Why was my mother so angry and so worried? Years later, I learned that the girl's father had probably cursed my mother and called her a German whore—or worse. Seven-year-old Venke was simply puzzled and hurt, but the incident exemplified the trauma that existed in Norway in the early post-war years.

Nazi Germany invaded the neutral, Scandinavian country of Norway in the spring of 1940. Within a month, it had

## Chapter One

conquered the peace-loving nation and swiftly and decisively established its rule. For five years, four hundred thousand German soldiers and six thousand members of the SS, the brutal Nazi organization that exterminated six million Jews throughout Europe, controlled everyday life in the country. A ratio of one German occupier for every eight Norwegian citizens kept the country firmly in the grip of the Nazis, who brutally stamped out any signs of resistance.

Not surprisingly, during the long occupation, thousands of local women fraternized with the invaders and gave birth to their children. Also, not surprisingly, these women and their offspring were reviled by the rest of the population. After the German surrender, in May 1945, many of the women were rounded up by their neighbors and publicly shamed; their heads were shaved and they were driven or dragged through the streets. Many were put to work, scrubbing and cleaning the vacated German barracks. "Cleaning out their shit," some called it. Many of the female collaborators were imprisoned at internment camps; others deported to Germany. Those who had become mothers were singled out, ostracized and humiliated, and branded as German whores and sluts; the children were despised as "Nazi spawn."

My mother was one of these women; I was one of the children. I never saw again the little girl in the neighborhood who was forbidden to play with me. My loose tongue had taught me a lesson. From then on, I clammed up. For the rest of my childhood I obeyed my mother and never again told anyone my father had been a German general, even though my birth certificate clearly stated: Father—General Heinrich Fehlis.

That incident carved an emotional scar I would carry for the rest of my life. I felt ashamed and guilty, although I didn't really know why. What was so wrong with my father being a general in the German army? He was a general, a high-ranking officer, not a lowly soldier. Why was my mother so distraught and alarmed? I was too young to understand anything more than it was a subject not to be discussed.

### The Russian Duke

In the years immediately after the war, when I was just a baby, my mother and I lived in Norway's neighbor to the east, Sweden, in the capital city of Stockholm. My earliest recollections are the 350-mile train trips I often made between Stockholm and Oslo where I had been born and where my mother's family lived. I loved the sound of the train's wheels going around and around as I drifted to sleep, tucked into my berth. I have no recollection of the scenic countryside that flashed by or the stations we stopped at, but I can still hear and feel the steady rhythm of the train chugging along the railway track.

In Sweden, my mother, whom everyone knew as Lillemor ("little mother"), a common nickname in Norway that she'd had since she was a little girl, managed to support the two of us by working at the local post office. She met and married a Russian duke, one of the thousands of Russian aristocrats who fled their country after the Bolsheviks seized power in 1917. The duke's name was Vladimir Matveev, but everyone simply called him "The Duke."

## Chapter One

In my eyes, he was a good-natured, elderly man with gray hair, although he probably wasn't older than fifty. Later, as a young girl, I read books in which Russian émigrés who had lost the lavish lifestyles they'd enjoyed in Moscow and St. Petersburg, were forced to eke out an existence as taxi drivers in cities like Paris and Rome. This duke—our duke—made his living as an actor. A real actor.

It was with him that I went to a movie theater for the first time and saw my first movie *Karleken Sagrar* (*Love Conquers All*). The duke had a small part in the movie; he played a poverty-stricken writer living in Vienna, Austria, who was arrested by the Germans and dispatched to a concentration camp because they considered his work anti-German. Sitting in the darkened theater, sandwiched between the duke and my mother, it was hard for me to fathom how he could be up there—on the big screen, larger than life—and yet sitting right next to me, too.

Lillemor and I lived with "The Duke" in a not-so-royal apartment that comprised one room and a kitchen area so cramped it could only accommodate one person at a time. The bathroom was no better. It was tiny, but it came with a hand-held shower. At least it was a real bathroom and it was luxurious compared with Mamma and Pappa's home in Oslo. There, I'd been bathed on the kitchen table in a tub filled with water that had been heated on the stove.

I was jealous of anyone who stole my mother's attention away from me. One day, when I was about four, I encountered her and the duke kissing in the hallway of our apartment. I was so mad at their display of affection that, without thinking, I kicked the duke's shin as hard as I could. They weren't pleased. For my punishment, I was locked in that tiny bathroom where my tantrum raged on. Defiantly, I grabbed that hand-held shower and sprayed the whole room.

Another time, my mother was invited to afternoon tea with some very nice, older ladies and took me along, dressed in my Sunday best. I sat next to her at a large, round table in a beautiful restaurant while the women kept saying "What a well-behaved little girl. How nice and quiet you are." It irritated me no end. So, I thought I'd show them just how quiet and well behaved I really was. I got off the chair and wriggled underneath the table, where no one could reach me, saying, "Kiss my ass. Kiss my ass." Swearing wasn't uncommon in our neighborhood, so I must have picked up the expression. It was terribly embarrassing for my mother and I don't think she was invited again. Apart from these incidents, I was generally an obedient little girl, or so I've been told.

I'd just turned seven when two life-altering events occurred. Lillemor was very attached to her father and was devastated when he was diagnosed with cancer of the mouth. She was, however, no longer so attached to the duke. She'd tired of him. It had never really been a love match and he hadn't been much of a provider, certainly not able to deliver the lifestyle I later learned my mother had enjoyed in Oslo during the war. As it was also time for me to attend grammar school, Lillemor peremptorily divorced the duke and moved us back home to Norway into the Tøyengata home of her ailing father and her mother.

# Chapter Two

My mother's father, Erling Schaug ("Pappa" to me), delivered milk with a horse and wagon. My mother's mother, Dagny (my "Mamma"), was a housewife. They both came from a small place in the county of Trøndelag in the center of Norway and brought to Oslo the area's characteristically dry sense of humor, a trait I inherited.

They were kind, thoughtful, wonderful grandparents. Unfortunately, though, Pappa had a problem with alcohol and every evening after work he arrived home a little the worse for wear. Mamma took comfort in her religion. She had a strong belief in God and took me to church with her. All the time. The church, which was housed in a building just around the corner from our home, was also a social center, a part of the local community, and I joined the girl scouts there.

Whenever there was something to be worried about, Mamma would say, "Fold your hands under the table and pray." That was her solution to every challenge. The other family members were not so religious and only bothered to attend "mandatory" celebrations such as Christmas and Easter. Lillemor was an out-and-out atheist, who even detested the sound of church bells. Many years later I discovered the reason for that.

As I mentioned, Lillemor had two sisters who lived with us. Her youngest sister, Berit, was fourteen years her junior and only seven years older than I, and Eva was two years younger than Lillemor and liked to play dolls with me. I always thought Tante Eva would have made the perfect mother for me; she was much more than an aunt, that's for sure. Relations between Lillemor and Tante Eva were always strained. Tante Eva had taken such good care of me during the times I visited with the family in Norway while Lillemor remained in Sweden, that Lillemor was jealous and threatened. Once, after Tante Eva had given me a bath and was holding me in her arms, Lillemor came into the room and snatched me away, declaring, "She's *my* daughter."

Below us, on the second floor, lived Britt, a girl my age, who became my first best friend. Together we spent time visiting an old lady who was paralyzed and housebound and who lived alone in an apartment on Britt's floor. I'm not sure it was our idea to be that altruistic. Our parents probably encouraged us to keep her company.

In our backyard was a small machine shop. Britt and I found it exciting to venture there and watch what the men were working on. They were a friendly group and got a kick out of the naïve curiosity of two little girls. The

## Chapter Two

world outside our apartment building was bursting with activity. Tøyengata was a very busy street with throngs of people energetically and noisily going about their lives and a streetcar loudly clanking as it passed by.

I remember hanging out of the third-story window looking at all of the hustle and bustle in the street down below. Often the police picked up people who'd been sleeping rough and threw them into a big black police van. Once I saw Mamma running down the street waving her large black umbrella above her head, screaming, "Police brutality! Police brutality!" She was quite a character.

Tøyengata boasted a butcher's shop, a fish market, a small general store on the corner and, further down, a candy store—as well as many other outlets providing everything the local residents could want. Directly across from our gate was Kjellands, a chocolate factory whose heavenly aroma sometimes drifted our way driving us crazy with desire.

My favorite was the general store. There, for the equivalent of a dime, I would buy a small paper cone filled with yeast and powdered sugar. I had my own secret tasting ritual. I'd scoop a little bit of yeast and put it in my mouth, followed by a little bit of powdered sugar. It had to be in that order—yeast and sugar—to get the flavorful taste sensation I craved.

In the summer months, all the children in the neighborhood spilled out onto the streets cycling up and down and playing games on the sidewalk. We swung on the bar of the heavy entrance gate to our building pretending we were Olympic gymnasts. In the winter, when it got bitterly cold, council workers sprayed water on the ground of our local park, magically transforming it for us into a temporary ice-skating rink.

The dark shadow over those days was Pappa's oral cancer. He suffered unbearable pain and, most of the time, was confined to bed, occasionally comforted by a visit from the priest. It was awful to see the right side of his face rotting away. Poor Pappa was unable to eat or drink. He could not even hold a cigarette in his mouth to satisfy a habit he could not quit and that had almost certainly caused the cancer. When Lillemor smoked, she inhaled the fumes deeply and blew them gently into Pappa's mouth so he could at least enjoy the taste of the tobacco. Pappa could not tolerate a lot of noise, so I tried to be as quiet as I could. I'd lie in bed next to him for hours, not moving an inch, wanting to comfort him.

At times, when he was in acute distress and needed complete quiet, my Tante Berit and I had to go stay with other family members. Thinking back, it was probably to spare me from witnessing the cruel progression of the cancer. We were all at my great-grandmother Schaug's house when Mamma came and broke the news that Pappa had died. After two years of agony, he'd finally been released. I locked myself in the bathroom to escape all the things I did not fully comprehend and could not change. It was a place of refuge for me.

### A New Stepfather

Lillemor was newly single. A beautiful young woman. And in great demand. I was jealous of the men she dated.

CHAPTER TWO

I screamed in protest every time someone came to the apartment to take her out on a date. I was afraid of losing her. And, of course, my fears were answered.

On a warm summer day on a beach in Oslo, eight years after Norway's liberation from Nazi Germany, she met Odd Fridtjof Gustafson. He'd joined the Freedom Fighters at a young age and was only eighteen when the Gestapo (**Ge**heime **Sta**ats**po**lizei), the feared Nazi secret police, arrested him for distributing leaflets in support of the Resistance and shipped him off to Sachsenhausen, a concentration camp in Oranienburg, just north of Berlin.

The camp mostly held political prisoners—men and women the Third Reich wanted in captivity, not because of their religion or ethnicity, but because of their political beliefs and power to speak up and influence others. It was a harsh existence. Like other labor camps, it had a gas chamber and a medical experimentation facility. Prisoners were given little food and were casually killed as their captors saw fit.

At Sachsenhausen, Odd became desperately ill and lost all his hair, and was only kept alive by the kindness of a German political prisoner. Ultimately, he was saved when the advancing Russian army, led by a female commander, liberated the camp on April 22, 1945. For the rest of his days Odd always spoke well of the Russian people.

When Odd entered the picture, I felt my life would never be the same. I was nine years old and growing tired of protesting my mother's endless stream of suitors, not that Lillemor paid much attention to my complaints. This time it was worse. Lillemor's relationship with Odd became serious and, in spite of my opposition, she accepted his proposal of marriage.

Bluntly, she told me, "I know you don't want me to get married again, but I am marrying Odd. And that's the end of it."

I felt numb. I had nothing to say anymore. There was no fight left in me. We moved out of Mamma and Pappa's small apartment in the city and into a place owned by Odd's stepfather in Lørenskog, a town about ten miles away. Our new home was a small one-bedroom cottage with an attic, and its best attribute was a large garden graced with fruit trees as well as wild blueberries and raspberries. When we were moving in, I couldn't help but notice a painting hanging prominently on the wall of the living room depicting a half-naked woman with sagging breasts. I thought it was strange, and it made me laugh. I was only nine years old and didn't know any better. It was just the honest, thoughtless reaction of a young girl.

"Ha. Ha. That's Lillemor," I said, pointing at the painting. I didn't mean to be hurtful but my mother looked at me, her face a mixture of pain and anger. Her breasts were not as firm as they used to be. I'd spoken the truth without considering the impact of my words.

"And that is *your* fault," she scolded. I never criticized her looks again.

I hated Odd from the beginning. He intimidated me from the first day I met him. He was physically imposing—6ft. 2in. tall, bald, skinny, and a bit scary looking. But

## Chapter Two

it went beyond his appearance. He behaved more like a mean, older stepbrother than a stepfather, a supposedly mature adult. He never physically hurt me, but he psychologically wounded me.

Odd delighted in degrading me and drawing attention to what he saw as my shortcomings and mistakes. If I seemed tired after mowing the grass he would say, in a sarcastic sing-song voice, "Look at Venke. Look how tired she is."

It may sound trite, but it was a relentless verbal beat-down, day after day.

I only have one good memory of Odd, and that was one of my birthdays when he hung candy on a string from the ceiling of my tiny bedroom. Lillemor never shielded me from his taunts. In some ways, she was just as bad. Once, I was in the car with the two of them and proudly showed her an essay I had written at school. She scoffed at my effort, and mockingly read it out loud placing exaggerated emphasis on words and phrases they thought were amusing. They both laughed. There was never any encouragement from either of them; quite the contrary.

They had a strange relationship. Odd had been incarcerated in a German concentration camp; my father had been a German officer. Odd's love for Lillemor must have enabled him to see past that dichotomy and accept that she was not responsible for Fehlis's actions. But it didn't stop him from sitting me on his lap one day, and stretching out his arms as if holding and aiming a rifle.

"Bang. Bang," he said menacingly. "Venke, this is how your father killed people. Lots of people."

I started to cry. Could this be true? Why was he saying that? Why was he being so mean? Why would he maintain that the father I'd never known had killed people—lots of people? Perhaps he realized he'd gone too far, as he changed his tone in an effort to console me. In a typical Odd mood switch, he said soothingly, "But, Venke, you are not like that."

Of course, I wasn't like that. I was a nine-year-old kid. But it was too late. The damage was done. It was the one and only time he ever spoke directly to me about my father. The war was never discussed. The subject was taboo in our house, even though the agony of those years still lived on in the lives of everyone in the country. My mother was so traumatized she would even get tense when German music played on the radio.

### The Household Battle

Odd and I constantly battled for my mother's attention. Odd usually won. Lillemor often told me how jealous he was, and that we had to be careful what we said to him because the years in the concentration camp had damaged him. Some inmates survived the camp only to kill themselves later, traumatized by what they had lived through; others became abusive alcoholics. That was Odd's affliction. He was a nasty drunk.

Lillemor also liked to drink to excess and, when they were drunk, they fought like cats and dogs, oblivious to my presence. My bedroom in the Lørenskog house was a small loft accessed by climbing a steep ladder from the kitchen.

## Chapter Two

Many nights I sat at the top of the ladder and listened to their drunken brawls, their shouting and cursing, and the sound of tables and chairs being overturned, crashing to the ground. During their fights, Odd goaded Lillemor claiming that my father had ruined his life.

"He signed the papers. He signed the papers that sent me to the camp!" I heard him scream, again and again. My mother was married to a man who'd been sent to his potential death in a concentration camp by her first husband? My young mind struggled to compute the claim and Odd and Lillemor's bizarre relationship. More than anything else, I was terrified Odd would seriously hurt her.

She made excuses for him: "He is not well, you understand."

Why were they together? Did she marry him just to get out of her parents' apartment? What kind of perverted bond did they have? Did she marry him out of guilt? Was she trying to atone for my father's involvement in the war? Or was it simply a true love match? Lillemor once tried to explain her marriage to Odd: "If he can forgive me, maybe the rest of Norway can forgive me." What on earth did she mean by that? Why would an entire country need to forgive her? It made no sense to me.

Odd was unstable; his moods unpredictable. He would be silent and morose for days while Lillemor and I sat quaking on the sofa waiting for the inevitable explosion. There was little joy in the home, especially on weekends and holidays. It was gray and sad and depressing. I was miserable and nervous all the time and figured there was something wrong with me. It began to manifest itself physically. I stammered and perspired heavily, staining my clothes. Worse still, I was bed-wetting, and the potential embarrassment prevented me from staying the night at friends' homes. It got so bad in my early teens that I was admitted into hospital for tests. Even more humiliating was the day a doctor pulled the sheet off my bed, exposing my naked body to the inquisitive eyes of a group of young male interns as I tried to cover my private parts. Unable to find a physical reason for my bedwetting, they simply sent me home.

After moving to Lørenskog I'd changed schools to be close to our new home, but I found it hard to make friends. It didn't help that Lillemor forced me do housework, even when I had a friend come to visit. Eventually, I returned to my old school near the apartment on Tøyengata and, after school was done for the day, often went to see Mamma. Lillemor and Odd would pick me up from there and take me back to Lørenskog.

## Chapter Three

When Odd was away from the house, Lillemor sometimes opened up about my father, telling me stories about how much in love they had been. This was our secret. Over and over again, I heard about their romance and their love; how happy they had been, and how they had wanted to have a daughter. I heard about the giddy side of their relationship—how once, standing on their bed, this usually severe military officer had jumped so high his head hit the ceiling.

"Why are you doing that?" she asked him.

"Because I am so happy I have you," he replied.

I heard about a man who was not only a loving father but who was also said to be a highly regarded general. Before the war, he had been a lawyer in Germany's high court. A fastidious military man who expected a clean white shirt every morning, he wanted her to remove his knee-high boots at night, something she adamantly refused to do.

I learned that, when I was born, Fehlis came to the hospital to pick us up and, so that his precious baby daughter would not be subjected to a draft, diligently applied tape all around the windows of the car to make sure there were no cracks. When I cried at night, it was Fehlis who got up to rock me back to sleep. He could not have been more caring and loving. He was as much the adoring, dutiful dad as he was the stern, disciplined military man.

Only once did Lillemor tell me a scary wartime story. She'd attended a dinner party with my father in honor of a high-ranking officer in the Gestapo, a man who was notorious for torturing prisoners. Lillemor told me she had looked at the man's hands and blurted, "How can such beautiful hands be so cruel!" It was not a smart thing to say to an individual whose day job was torturing and killing. My father was taken aback and, when they were alone, warned her that if she'd made such an outrageous statement in Germany, instead of Norway, he would not have been able to protect her. Another time she told me my father had twice gone to Berlin to ask to be released from his position, and, on the second occasion, he had taken her with him. It didn't add up that a general would seek such a transfer but I was too young to know that, and merely absorbed the stories she told me and the picture she painted of their life together and with me.

Lillemor also regaled me with accounts about Tante Gerd, as we called her. Gerd Høst Heyerdahl was a famous Norwegian actress. Lillemor had met her in Norway during

## Chapter Three

the war and came into contact with her again in Sweden soon after the conflict had ended. I loved to hear Lillemor talk about Gerd as I stared wide-eyed at the photos she had of Gerd on stage. My favorite photo was of Gerd dressed as an angel for a performance at the Royal Theatre. Tante Gerd, who had spent time in Germany and spoke the language fluently, also gave German language lessons on the radio, and I listened totally entranced by the voice of this angel.

In the years we lived at Lørenskog, when Odd was absent from the home, Lillemor dribbled out other snippets of information about her earlier life. She told me that when she returned to Norway from Sweden, she had been arrested on the train and then transported to a prison camp and interrogated while I was placed in the care of relatives.

Her inquisitors demanded to know how she had managed to get out of Norway at the close of the war and enter Sweden. Who had helped her cross the border that was supposedly closed? Whom had she lived with in Stockholm? They grilled her. For three weeks, she was questioned and she didn't divulge anything. Then they let her go. Lillemor also told me about a Swedish family, the Södermans, that had been really kind to her when she lived in Stockholm, and treated her like one of their own.

### YOU HAVE A BROTHER

One day, when I was about nine or ten years old, Lillemor instructed me to sit with her at the kitchen table. There was something she wanted to tell me about her relationship with my father.

# Venke

The way she asked me to sit down was unusually formal. I sensed there was going to be something different about this conversation, that she wanted to make an announcement, and that she was building up to a revelation of some kind. She was physically shaking. Nervous about this unusual turn of events, I also began to tremble as she took a deep breath and briskly declared:

"Venke, I have to tell you something. You have a brother. In Germany. One day you will get to meet him and the rest of his family."

I had a brother? In Germany? Open-mouthed, I stared at her in disbelief. I couldn't speak.

"You might have an older sister, as well."

A brother? *Maybe* a sister? Even more family? It was too much to take in. For all these years, I'd had no reason to think I was anything other than the only child of a wartime romance that had somehow come to an end when the war was over. Totally confused, I stammered, trying to collect my thoughts and ask the obvious questions that were swirling inside my head.

But as quickly as she'd begun the mind-boggling revelation, Lillemor stopped. I guess my stunned reaction and my look of astonishment had given her pause. She abruptly quit talking.

"That's all I wanted to tell you. That's all I'm going to say."

She got up and walked away. The conversation was over. I couldn't question her. That was not the kind of relationship we had. It was another secret between the two of us. It was part of our life, and Odd was excluded. It became

## Chapter Three

an unspoken, taboo subject, something that could only ever be discussed again if and when Lillemor was good and ready. It was an amazing revelation firmly etched in my mind, never to be forgotten. A revelation that raised more questions and tormented me for years to come.

## Chapter Four

I was growing up fast—physically, anyway. Puberty for me started much earlier than it did for other girls in my gym glass. When we showered, they made fun of me, pointing at my budding breasts and laughing. I explained my predicament to Lillemor and she wrote a note to the school excusing me from gym. She continued writing those notes for about two years, but we never spoke about it again. We never had a mother-daughter talk. She never explained what it meant to become a woman. Worried that Odd would torment me, I tried to hide my developing breasts by binding a scarf around my chest.

In 1955, five years after moving into the cottage in Lørenskog, we had to leave because Odd's stepfather needed to sell the place. We moved back to Oslo to a small apartment on Eiriks Gata in the Tøyen neighborhood. It had a kitchen, a hallway, a bathroom, a bedroom, and an

## Chapter Four

alcove. I was fourteen and started high school. It's an awkward age for any girl, and I was acutely aware how shabby I looked compared with my classmates. I wore ill-fitting hand-me-downs from my mother; most of the other girls were smartly turned out in brand new school clothes. I was also tall and gawky—even taller than all the boys my age. And with my kinky hair, pale skin, and my light eyebrows and eyelashes, I felt acutely out of place, as if I were an outsider peering into a world of privilege ... an ugly duckling among so many swans. I was convinced I was ugly.

My grandmother inadvertently made it worse by telling me how beautiful Lillemor had been as a young girl, so beautiful that boys would line up outside the apartment hoping for a date with her. It was tough to hear about the beauty of my mother when I did not look at all like her. Presumably, I'd inherited my father's looks, although right then I didn't know what he looked like. The last thing I wanted was to make myself visible. I preferred to stay in the shadows and secretly watch with envy the cute girls in the schoolyard.

Luckily, I was befriended by two nice girls who lived on my street. They introduced me to a ballroom dancing school called Bårdar, which I loved. For five years, I went there every chance I got while fantasizing about become a ballerina and the ugly duckling morphing into a beautiful swan. I would probably have become a professional dancer, if only I'd got a little encouragement at home, but Lillemor and Odd were too preoccupied drinking and brawling and had no time for me and my aspirations.

### Not OK to Cry

Lillemor was not a typical mother. She was never "mom" to me. Like everyone else, I always called her Lillemor, not mom. She didn't care about my appearance or the emotional teenage growing pains I experienced. On the contrary, she could be cold and hard.

She didn't appreciate my emotional reaction to movies and TV shows that left her untouched. In a movie theater during a showing of *Heidi*, a musical about an orphan, played by Shirley Temple, who was forced to live as a companion to a spoiled, crippled girl, I wept so much that Lillemor, embarrassed and angry, dragged me out of the theater. The same thing happened when we went to see the Oscar-winning drama, *How Green Was My Valley*.

When I was about sixteen, we watched a German operetta together on television. I was so touched by the story that I cried and cried. Lillemor was unmoved. After I'd gone to bed that night she came into my room, sat on the bed and pointedly told me, "Venke, the only people who cry are those who feel sorry for themselves." What mother tells her daughter it's never OK to cry?

We lived in Eiriks Gata for just two years before we moved to a place called Høyenhal where I finished high school (the Norwegian equivalent of two years of college in the U.S.). Upon graduation, I got a job in the accounts payable department at A/S Volvo, the car manufacturer Everything was all right for a while, except at home. The relationship with Lillemor and Odd was frayed and continued to deteriorate.

## Chapter Four

One evening, when I arrived home, Odd was drunk—and naked—in the living room, sprawled in his armchair staring morosely at the flickering television. He turned and looked at me without making any effort to cover himself. I rushed upstairs and into my bedroom, noticing on the way that Lillemor was passed out on the bed in her room. Breathless and shaken, I locked my bedroom door. Thank God, Odd did not try anything because I don't know how I would have reacted, but I felt more ill at ease and vulnerable than ever in that apartment.

The next day, when my mother and I were standing in the kitchen doing the dishes, I tried to tell her what had happened and anxiously blurted out, "Lillemor, guess what Odd did last night?" She didn't want to know. She didn't care. She deliberately turned her head—away from me—and didn't say a word. The unspoken message was crystal clear. She just didn't want to have a conversation about it, whatever *it* was. It was a situation she didn't want to address.

### Life in London

I had to get away from this toxic environment. Luckily, my girlfriend Marit had worked as an au pair in London and knew of a family that was looking for someone. So, just after my seventeenth birthday, at the end of January 1962, I traveled to London to take up a one-year position with a really nice family. Well, at least they appeared to be nice at first. Marit came over a couple of months later and we got together on my day off with a couple of guys she knew who were students. They gave us a tour of their college and we had something to eat, and then I realized it was so late I wouldn't be able to catch the last train home.

One of the boys stepped up and gave me a ride. Which was fine, except we got lost. Neither of us knew exactly how to get to the address where I lived. He was upset. I was upset. And things got worse when we stopped at a police station to ask for directions. I'd been reported as missing! My good Samaritan was livid at the situation he'd been dragged into, but offered to explain to the family what had happened. I didn't want any more help. I was so angry I jumped out of his car slamming the door behind me, not paying attention to the fact that the ground was icy. I slipped and fell flat on my face. When my hosts opened the front door of their house, they found me looking a terrible mess. They were not sympathetic and I was fired the next day.

I soon managed to get another position as an au pair with a family of Orthodox Jews. That was quite an experience. Living with them was so different from anything a seventeen-year-old girl in Tøyengata had ever known. The kitchen was split in half: one side, complete with appliances, sink, and dishes, was for meat; the other side was for dairy. The two halves could not, under any circumstances, be mixed together. If that happened (as it did once), the dishes that had been contaminated were buried in the backyard for a few days. After a couple of months, I'd had enough of life as an au pair in London and managed to persuade Lillemor to send me a ticket for a ferry ride back to Norway.

# Chapter Five

Lillemor and Odd had relocated again. They were living in an apartment that came with Odd's new job as a custodian at Handelsgymnasiet, a university in Oslo. I got a job as a receptionist for a temporary agency and fell in love with my first serious boyfriend. His name was Helge. He was tall, blond and, as far as I was concerned, very good-looking.

Helge was a member of the Royal Guards whose sole duty was to protect the Royal Palace and, since the palace was in the heart of Oslo, we were able to see a lot of each other. We dated for two years and became engaged, although his parents weren't too happy. Helge was twenty-one; I was nineteen. His parents felt we were too young and I suspect they also thought I wasn't good enough for him. When he broke up with me, I was devastated. I thought he was as much in love with me as I was with him, but he wasn't. Years later,

VENKE

I got a letter from him confessing that he'd really been in love with my girlfriend, Jorun. If that was the case, why the hell did he ever ask me to marry him?

I'd met Jorun at a summer camp in Hovedøya in the countryside near Oslo when I was about thirteen or fourteen. After that, we were together all the time. She was a charming brunette who had no problem finding boyfriends. Boys were crazy about her while they tended to ignore me. I felt like a third wheel when I went out with Jorun and one of her boyfriends. Once, walking down the street in Tøyen, I told her that my mother had been enthusing about a new girl who was working with her at her latest office job. It was strange. Wherever she worked, Lillemor seemed to befriend a young girl closer to my age than hers.

Jorun, who was aware of this, turned to me and declared, "Lillemor needs to show less interest in the girls she works with, and more with what's going on with you!"

It was a strong, revealing statement about my relationship with my mother that has stayed with me ever since.

Somehow, Odd managed to get a job as a security guard at the Munch Museum in Oslo, the institution dedicated to the life and works of Norway's most famous artist, Edvard Munch, whose best-known work is *The Scream*. I have no clue how Odd got the job in the first place and it shocked me that he remained employed as he was in a drunken stupor most of the time. The position came with a very nice apartment and an impressive uniform, which Odd loved to wear.

CHAPTER FIVE

## THE PICTURE IN THE HALL

At home one day I was astonished to see that Lillemor had hung a picture of my father in the hallway, a small, framed copy of a newspaper photo. Why she did that I have no idea. Why Odd didn't have a problem with it, I also don't know. Hanging in his hallway in pride of place was a picture of a man who he claimed had sent him to a concentration camp where he could easily have died. What man would allow that? A few evenings later, Lillemor and Odd were both standing in the hallway looking at the picture as I walked by. Odd made a great show of staring at the picture, and then looked directly at me, and said to both of us, "Venke looks so much like her father, especially around the mouth." I didn't take it as a compliment as Fehlis has been described as having "thin, bloodless lips."

During those days, there were other reminders of my mother's past relationship with a German officer. My grandmother confided that shortly after the liberation, a group of people arrived at her door looking for Lillemor. They knew she'd been involved with a German and wanted to punish her by shaving her head. But Lillemor and I were already safely in Sweden. Lillemor herself, in one of our "secret" kitchen chats, revealed that she'd been subjected to a verbal affront when she was first back in Norway and working as a bookkeeper at A/S Buckholtz, a men's suit manufacturing company. A fabric salesman recognized her and asked a room full of people in a loud, accusatory voice, "Are you aware she's a German whore?"

Lillemor was mortified, but her coworkers rallied around her, shoved the man's fabrics back into his suitcase, and strong-armed him out of the building. By this time, the stigma of having had a relationship with a German soldier was forgiven by many Norwegians—especially the young men who continued to find Lillemor's beauty irresistible. Lillemor brushed aside the salesman's denouncement of her and was proud that her friends at work had stood up for her.

She wasn't so proud when I came home one day in January, 1965, and found her at the kitchen table, with her head buried in her hands. She was trembling, a nervous wreck.

"Lillemor," I asked, "what's the matter? What's happened?"

There had been a story on the news about a high-ranking Gestapo officer, Hellmuth Reinhard, who'd served in Norway during the war and, twenty-four years later, had just been sentenced in Germany to five years' imprisonment as an accessory to murder. He was said to be partly responsible for the deportation of at least five hundred thirty-two Norwegian Jews. He'd gone underground at the end of the war and had been able to escape capture and punishment—until now. Why was Lillemor so upset? He had been a friend of my father and a witness at their wedding, she explained. This news story had a greater impact on her than anything I'd ever witnessed before.

Odd became more isolated and distant. He seemed nervous, on edge all the time. He went days without saying a word to either Lillemor or me, sitting in sullen silence, ignoring both of us. When he did talk, he was argumentative and spoiling for a fight. Their relationship made my life unbearable. Most of the time they paid no attention to me. There was no love or caring. I was a visible reminder of the ugly past, of my mother's sin with Fehlis. My presence kindled Odd's jealousy. Both of them continued to drink heavily. Alcohol was their refuge. They were two damaged people unable to cope with their own lives, never mind care about mine.

**FAMILY FEUD**

My mother's relationships with Mamma and Tante Eva were also fraught with difficulties. Lillemor resented the way she felt she'd been treated by her mother and her sister. In the aftermath of the war, when she'd been living in Sweden, which had not suffered the deprivations of Norway, she sent food and clothing back to the family because rationing was still in force. But she never got so much as a thank you, she claimed. She was hurt and couldn't put it behind her. She'd even sent her baby sister, Berit, a small bicycle and, when Berit got too big for it, it was just the right size for me. But Lillemor said she had to pay her mother to regain possession of the bike, something she would never forget or forgive.

It was hard for me to hear all this, because I loved Mamma so much. Lillemor, though, wanted me to know the not-so-likeable side of Mamma; she wanted to build a wall between us. She even told me that, during one of their fights, when we first lived with her immediately after the war, Mamma had said to her, "You and your bastard baby get out of here." Why would she say such a thing? Why would she say I was a bastard? I was devastated. So many things didn't make sense.

A way to escape presented itself. Tante Berit, who'd been living in America and now had a family on Staten Island, suggested I move there. It was the summer of 1965. I was twenty. And it was a golden opportunity. But even my departure from Norway was tinged with the kind of melodrama I'd come to expect. The night before I was due to leave, I was already in bed when Lillemor came into my room and sat on the edge of the bed. We chit-chatted for a while about the adventure I was about to undertake and then, before she got up to leave, she said cryptically, "You know Venke, sometimes it's OK to tell a white lie."

That was it. No further explanation. This was so typical of my mother. No doubt there was a deeper meaning, but nothing Lillemor cared to share with me. What on earth was the white lie?

## Chapter Six

My fresh beginning in America got off to a rocky start. Tante Berit knew of a family in New Canaan, Connecticut, that was looking for an au pair. The plan was that I would work for the Alpers family for a year, while improving my English, and then apply to become a Pan Am stewardess—that's what we called female flight attendants back then. Berit knew that my home life with Lillemor and Odd was miserable and that it had been further derailed when Helge broke up with me. It was definitely time to begin again . . . 3,700 miles away.

Within a week of my arrival, I knew I'd made a big mistake. Not only was I homesick, but I was also being unfairly treated by the host family. I'd been led to believe that my primary responsibility would be to help take care of their three children—the typical au pair role—but, as soon as I got there, I was handed three pages of handwritten notes dictating all the household duties expected of me. With barely time to settle in, I was set to work scrubbing floors and sent down to the basement to wash and iron clothes. I was being treated like a maid and not an au pair. Regardless, I decided to tough it out.

It helped when I met Mario Devivo—before the end of that first week.

That came about because Mrs. Alpers called the YMCA to ask if there were other European girls in the neighborhood and arranged for me to get together with some other au pairs, one from the Netherlands and twins from Switzerland. The four of us caught the train into New York to go shopping and, that evening, back in Connecticut, we went dancing at the German club. That's when and where Mario entered my life. He was a little taller than I, and a typical good-looking Italian, slim, and dark. Quite a contrast to my pale-skinned, blond, blue-eyed Scandinavian look.

He asked me out to dinner, and then for another date. On the third occasion, we double-dated with another couple who were friends of his. I wasn't used to drinking, but Mario ordered drink after drink and, somehow, I managed to consume seven Manhattans. I must have felt I was being so adult but the whiskey and vermouth concoction had the predictable effect. I was so ill that, on the way home, he had to pull the car over so I could throw up. He stood behind me saying, in his thick Italian accent, "Jesus Christ! Jesus Christ!" Well, what did he expect? He was the one who plied me with all the alcohol. He wasn't at all

## Chapter Six

sympathetic, and that should have been my first clue.

Most of my family in Norway were heavy drinkers, but alcohol had never appealed to me. That began to change. I began to like the taste and the effect. Mario and I were seeing each other all the time, and he wanted to take it to the next level; he wanted more than friendship. I wasn't ready for that, but, when I tried to break up with him, he got angry, grabbed my chin and pinched my cheek so hard it hurt for hours. I refused to see him but he kept calling and begging. Mrs. Alpers knew what was going on and told me that I didn't have to talk to him, but I was so unhappy and homesick I relented. At least meeting him for dinner and drinks (which I enjoyed) got me out of their house. About six months later, Mario and I became intimate. I guess I felt I owed sex to him after all the time we'd spent together. Within three months, I was pregnant.

When I came out of the doctor's office and confirmed my suspicions, Mario looked angry, especially, I think, because I looked happy.

"Why are you smiling?" he snarled at me.

Deep down, I sensed it was the best thing that could ever happen to me. A sign from the Universe, although I have to admit I briefly considered and rejected the idea of an abortion. Thank God.

But first we had to break the news to our parents. Having a child outside of marriage was scandalous in those days, and Mario's mother didn't take it too well (his father had died when the family still lived in Italy). I sat outside their house while Mario told her. She screamed so loud I thought the roof would collapse. A burst of Italian, a loud barrage of rapid-fire words could be heard all the way out on the sidewalk. I couldn't understand a word, although I definitely got the meaning. The way she and the rest of the family looked at me was a nightmare. I was the gold-digger from Norway.

I phoned Lillemor to tell her, not knowing what to expect. Her reaction couldn't have been more different. She acted like it was no big deal her young daughter had moved to America and got herself pregnant.

"Just do what you have to do," she said.

Lillemor's indifference should not have been a surprise.

Should I get married and have the baby? Tante Berit persuaded me that it was the right thing to do. Although I wasn't at all religious, to keep Mario's Italian family happy, we had a proper Catholic wedding with one hundred fifty guests, nearly all of them from his side of the family. I didn't convert to Catholicism but had to agree that the child would be raised in the Catholic faith.

After the wedding, we honeymooned in Norway so I could introduce my new husband to my family. That's when Mario and Lillemor butted heads for the first, but not the last, time. The issue was money. I'd been sending money back home for Lillemor to save for me, but it was all gone. She said they'd had to spend it to cover basic household bills and living expenses. I think it more likely it was spent on liquor. Mario was furious and never stopped complaining that my money was gone, even after we returned to the States. I wasn't happy about it, either, but

CHAPTER SIX

I couldn't understand why he was so angry. Did he think I should have come with a dowry or something?

## THE ITALIAN FAMILY

Mario was one of eight siblings, four girls and four boys, in a very old-fashioned Italian family. Every Sunday they had the big traditional family dinner. It started at 2:00 p.m. and went late into the night. The first one I attended—well before we were married—was a culture shock. Everyone at the table talked animatedly in Italian, expressing themselves with lots of energetic arm- and hand-waving. I couldn't understand any of it. It was torture. All the relatives were emotional and cried a lot, wailing about family members they missed who were still back in Italy.

But that's the southern Italians for you, and such a contrast to my cold and rigid upbringing in Norway and Sweden. There was one occasion when the dinner table went quiet and I realized they were all staring at me. Perhaps I'd been the topic of conversation. Perhaps someone had asked me a question and I didn't know what they were saying. I felt the blood quickly rise up my neck and spread across my face—blushing had always been a problem for me.

To overcome my nerves and discomfort my solution was to resort to alcohol. They served homemade wine and I didn't like the taste. I'd never drunk wine before and didn't know if it was good or bad, but it felt very soothing when it hit my stomach. So, I took a good few sips. Every time the carafe was passed around the table, I pushed my glass forward for a refill. That was the only way I seemed to be able to get through the dinner and I began to use alcohol as a crutch, something that would almost destroy me in later years.

Seven months pregnant, I'd had enough of these family dinners. One Sunday I declared, "I'm sick and tired of sitting there for hours while your family jabbers on in Italian and I don't know what they're saying. And they're all staring at me. I've had enough. I'm not going."

I locked myself in the bathroom. I thought I was safe and secure and there was nothing he could do about it. He'd have to go by himself. Mario was furious.

"You're going whether you like it or not. You're my wife and you're going."

Somehow, he took the hinges off the door, hit me on the head, grabbed my arm and dragged me out. I was forced to attend dinner and not say a word about the assault—an indication of things to come. Otherwise, my pregnancy was uneventful, and I had an easy time of it. The labor was fast, though painful. Joseph Mario arrived on January 25, 1967, weighing 7lbs. 2oz. I had no say in naming our baby boy. Joseph was the obvious choice because Mario's father was called Joseph and, of course, Mario had to get himself in there as well. Mario and his family would have never entertained the German name Heinrich, even if I'd pushed for it. So, my son became Joseph Mario.

It wasn't long before he was just Joe. I'd started calling him Joey but with my Norwegian accent it sounded like Joe-vee and our neighbors and Joe's friends made fun of me. Joe it remained. I could say that to everyone's satisfaction.

# Chapter Six

After two years of marriage, Mario decided that our two-bedroom apartment in Norwalk, Connecticut, wasn't good enough, and we bought a home in a new residential area in the nearby town of Bethel. It was a wonderful place to raise Joe—plenty of space where children could play, and lots of neighborhood parties. We grilled in our backyards when the weather was fine and we grilled in our garages when it rained.

In public, we appeared to be the perfect family. An upwardly mobile couple living the American dream. Behind closed doors it was a different story. Mario became increasingly jealous and abusive, both verbally and physically. He found fault with everything: the way I dressed, the meals I cooked, the opinions I expressed. He was especially mean to Lillemor every time she came to visit, and their mutual animosity increased over the years. They clashed all the time—probably because they both vied to be in control of me. In spite of that, when Mario and I fought, as we often did, Lillemor never defended me.

"Why don't you stand up for me?" I asked her. "He's got his whole family here on his side."

"Oh, I can't. I'm the mother-in-law," was all she replied.

When we first met, I'd told Mario my father had been a German general and that didn't sit well with him, although, of course, Germany and Italy had been allies in World War II. Once, when Lillemor was visiting from Norway, he got into a row with her and, in front of his whole family, called her a German whore.

One of his sisters reprimanded him, "Mario, don't speak like that. She is Venke's mother."

But Mario was unrepentant. When I pointed out that Italy under Mussolini fought on the side of the Germans, he was dismissive, saying, "Oh, no. That was just a misunderstanding."

About three years after our wedding Lillemor came on another visit. She had barely unpacked her suitcase before handing a recent edition of a large broadsheet to me—*Verdens Gang*, one of the main Norwegian newspapers.

"Here," she said, without any preamble. "Read about your father."

My father? Why would they be writing about my father twenty-four years after his death and the end of the war? What could be so newsworthy? The article was spread across the two center pages of the newspaper. A large photograph of my father in uniform stared back at me. The lantern jaw. The thin lips. But, most of all, the deep penetrating eyes that seemed to see right through me.

The banner headline declared: "The Horse Trade."

I gripped the paper in both hands and sank into a chair at the kitchen table. The article was all about my father, Heinrich Fehlis, my mother—and me! Information that had been a closely guarded secret locked away in Norwegian government files and marked not to be opened for twenty-four years was finally made public. I learned facts that Lillemor had never seen fit to share with me. Now she was doing so, but through the medium of a newspaper article. I learned some dramatic details about my unwitting part in an historical and previously unreported event. Twenty-four years after the fact.

## Chapter Seven

The war was over. Hitler had committed suicide in his Berlin bunker on April 30, 1945. Germany officially surrendered on May 8. The conditions included the arrest and internment of all Nazi party members and SS troops—the Schutzstaffel, one of the most powerful and feared Nazi organizations—as well as the surrender of all regular army troops. It was an uncertain time.

There were more than four hundred thousand troops in Norway and six thousand members of the SS. There were also thousands of members of the Norwegian state police and others who had worked for the Germans, actively collaborating with them to subjugate their fellow citizens.

Would they all lay down their arms peacefully? The underground Resistance only had four hundred thousand members with another thirteen thousand armed Norwegians across the border in Sweden trained and ready to reenter their homeland. What chance would they have if the overwhelming force of Germans and their Norwegian sympathizers ignored the surrender and decided to fight on?

According to the *Verdens Gang* account, written by the paper's editor, Oskar Hasselknippe, my father had been actively involved in secret negotiations brokered by Swedish police chief Harry Söderman, designed to avoid confrontation between the opposing forces. Söderman, who reveled in the nickname "Revolver Harry," had initiated talks with the German leadership in Norway because he was worried about the safety of Norwegian prisoners who were under the control of the SS, and because there had been threats the Germans would fight to the last man. It was well known that Reichskommissar Josef Terboven, the German overlord in Norway, wanted to make the country the last bastion of Hitler's Third Reich—a "Fortress Norway" (Festung Norvegen). Rumors swirled that the Nazis would not capitulate, and would fight on, as the maniacal Terboven wished. The huge German armed forces, including numerous detachments with fresh combat experience on the Northern Front in Russia and Finland, were a dire threat. It was entirely possible that thousands of prisoners held by the Germans could easily be executed in revenge.

For his part, Fehlis was concerned about the safety of his men in the aftermath of the bitter war. Would there be reprisals? How would they be treated? Would they be regarded as prisoners of war or summarily executed?

CHAPTER SEVEN

Fehlis had responded to Söderman's overtures and, a few weeks earlier on April 22, 1945, crossed the border into Sweden to meet with him for the first time, while an entire German battalion remained hidden in the woods on the Norwegian side. During a day of negotiations in the small border town of Charlottenberg, Fehlis gave the impression he was acting under the authority of Reichskommissar Terboven and that details of the meeting would also be passed on to Heinrich Himmler, one of Hitler's top cronies and the infamous head of the SS (the SS ran the death camps). At the end of the meeting, as they stood at the border crossing, Fehlis opened a bottle of cognac. The two men clinked tiny glasses toasting to the success of their negotiations and shared a farewell drink. Söderman felt he had established a bold and imperative working rapport and an understanding with the German.

Anxious to reach a resolution, Söderman called Fehlis every other day to see if Himmler had granted permission for their discussions to continue, but there had been no response. What Söderman didn't know was that Terboven was furious when Fehlis reported details of the meeting to him. He was so enraged he even accused Fehlis of treason and threatened to arrest him. Terboven was a hardliner, an extremist who had not weakened in his desire for the German army to continue to fight in disregard of the supreme order of the German leadership.

By Saturday, May 5, Fehlis took it upon himself to suggest to Söderman that he travel to Norway so discussions could continue. Söderman took the night train to the

— 43

Swedish-Norwegian border, where a car was waiting to transport him to a meeting at a large villa commandeered by the Germans after its shipbuilder owner fled to England.

After a sumptuous midday meal, negotiations resumed. The newspaper reported that, according to Söderman, Fehlis seemed to think the prisoners he held in the Norwegian prisons could be used as bargaining pawns. He had the attitude that he could let some go and he could keep others as hostages. Their lives were in his hands. Söderman worried that the Germans might not relinquish power peacefully and he desperately wanted to avoid further bloodshed.

It was May 6. Anything could happen. The war was officially at an end, but now was as dangerous a time, maybe more dangerous, than ever. Söderman was anxious to broker a deal to get Norwegian prisoners transferred to Sweden and also secure a guarantee of safety for the one hundred thousand Russian prisoners held in the north of Norway.

A meeting between Fehlis and Terboven was scheduled for the next day, but Germany's capitulation overtook negotiations and the meeting was canceled. Instead, Fehlis drove alone to Skaugum, the former residence of the crown prince of Norway that Terboven had seized for his personal living quarters. Knowing that it was all over, as he no longer had the power to force soldiers in Norway to fight on, Terboven ordered Fehlis to join him in a suicide pact. Fehlis refused.

Late that day, as it became increasingly obvious the German reign was finished, Söderman secretly met with

Fehlis again. Fehlis was willing to cooperate and hand over the keys to the prison at Grini in the suburbs of Oslo where five thousand prisoners were held, but he wanted something in return. According to the newspaper account, the quid pro quo was that Söderman would take care of a certain lady and her daughter, Fehlis's love child, and smuggle them out, unharmed, to the safe haven of neutral Sweden. This was the "horse trade" to which the newspaper article referred.

**CROSSING THE BORDER**

That was how, at the age of three months, I was handed by Fehlis to Lillemor sitting in the back seat of a big, black, chauffeur-driven, government car as it idled outside their Oslo residence. In the back with Lillemor was Söderman. The journey to the border was uneventful, but crossing into Sweden was a risk, even for someone as powerful as Söderman. We had neither passports nor visas and had no legitimate right to enter the country.

As we approached the border, my mother huddled me close to her chest as we lay hidden under a blanket. Our freedom depended on the border guards, who were well aware that the end of the war could spur an exodus of collaborators and who were likely to be more rigorous than ever when scrutinizing anyone seeking to cross. Luckily, the presence of Söderman was enough for the car to be waved through the checkpoint without being searched.

This newspaper account thrust into my hands by my mother was how I discovered why I spent the first few years of my life in Sweden rather than Norway. I sat shell shocked in the kitchen of my beautiful American home 3,700 miles away from Oslo and twenty-four years away from the end of the war. I stared at the formal portrait of my father. I read and reread the article. Parts of it had been neatly cut out, but I didn't question why, and it would be years before I discovered the disturbing information that was missing.

I wondered why Lillemor was showing me this article. Was it because she thought I might see it, anyway, that someone else might send it to me? Or did she want me to have a better understanding of what it had been like for her, my father, and for me? If so, why had she never discussed it before? Even now, she didn't want to talk about it. It was typical of the way Lillemor had always half-shared vital information. I should have insisted on knowing more. But I didn't. That was the nature of our relationship and, in this case, she made it clear she wanted the newspaper story to speak for itself.

All Lillemor said was, "I thought you'd like to know."

End of discussion.

## Chapter Eight

Mario and I were classic examples of what it meant to live the American dream: two European immigrants who returned from our honeymoon with twenty dollars between the two of us. He had no education; he'd only completed three years of primary school. His command of the English language was poor. I spoke English somewhat better, having learned it in school and through real-world experience when I was an au pair in London. But what we had going for us was that we both had a strong work ethic.

Mario and his brother, Armando, bought a failing business with $3,000 they had saved. The business manufactured side loader garbage trucks but Mario turned it into a remarkable success by making metal containers for refuse. I will say this for Mario: he had a great head for business and worked hard, although he became consumed by the business. I handled the finances using our kitchen table as my office. I'll never forget the day Mario came home waving a letter from the IRS with a tax bill the company had inherited from the previous owner.

"Venke, it's all over," he said, handing the letter to me. "They want $5,000."

I studied it. He'd misread it.

"Mario, it's $500 not $5,000. It's not that bad."

We could afford to pay that amount and keep the IRS off our backs. Dealing with people in the garbage industry was a tough business especially when it came to making sure you got paid. Once, when Mario was trying to collect a debt, one guy opened his desk drawer to pointedly reveal a handgun. Nevertheless, Mario managed to get paid—it was hard to scare him—but he acquired a valuable lesson.

He told me, "Venke, I'll never deal with anyone from the Bronx again."

The building that housed our manufacturing operation in Norwalk, Connecticut, was in terrible condition and too small for our mushrooming needs. On top of that, Mario worked until late at night. Sometimes he wouldn't get home until 11:00 p.m. So, after six years living in Bethel, he decided to build a new factory on a small piece of industrial land he'd found in Norwalk. The only way to finance the factory was to sell our home. Which was fine with me because moving to Norwalk meant I would be close to my dearest friend, Wenche.

Wenche and I had met in nearby Stamford in 1966 when we were both riding an elevator to the passport

CHAPTER EIGHT

office. I was pregnant and she had her little boy, Steven, in her arms. Once we realized we were both Norwegian, we exchanged phone numbers and were soon getting together regularly.

By the time the new factory was ready, Armando and their oldest brother Tony, who was also involved in the business, wanted to return to Italy, so Mario bought Armando's share of the company. As well as selling our home, we'd had to take out large loans to build the place, but Mario had met a banker willing to take a chance on him, a man whose father had immigrated from Ireland and whose work ethic had made a lasting impression on the son. Mario reminded him of his father. When we opened the factory, I gave up the kitchen table for an elegantly furnished office with large windows at the manufacturing plant. Mario was "thoughtful" when it came to material considerations and projecting the right kind of image: he wanted his wife to work in style, and all he really cared about was business, business, business. The downside of having the beautiful office was that Mario and I were together 24/7.

Two years later, thanks to the growing success of the business, we bought a three-acre plot of land in Wilton, Connecticut, a prosperous small town, which reminded me of Norway. We could afford to buy the land; the cost of building our custom home was something else, but, with the help of Italian craftsmen friends, we made it happen.

Soon after moving in, my son Joe, out riding his bike, met a neighbor lady who, he said, "spoke funny" just like

— 49

I did. Sure enough, Turi Josefsen was also from Norway. Turi and her husband Leon, who'd made a fortune designing and manufacturing surgical instruments, owned the adjoining one hundred twenty acres of property, which boasted two lakes. They didn't build there—they used it as a recreation area. Turi and Leon lived fifteen minutes away, in Westport, and we soon became great friends. I went on to develop an especially close relationship with Turi's mother, a beautiful, slender lady, who was always smartly dressed, and visited often from Norway.

## An Unhappy Marriage

Life could have been good. We had many Norwegian friends in the area, a lot of them in the shipping industry. It was a "high society" life—parties, boat trips, dinners, and more parties. We had a large, stunning, contemporary-style house with high ceilings, three bedrooms, three fireplaces, an open kitchen with family room, a large freestanding television, a gym, a finished basement with a built-in wet bar, and a large balcony overlooking a swimming pool. I drove a blue Porsche 928 GT. We had everything we had dreamed of, everything we could have possibly wanted—except a happy marriage.

In all honesty, I was never in love with Mario. Never. I married him because I got pregnant. That's what you did in those days. We had some good times together, and he was generous. But most of the time he was verbally and emotionally abusive. He berated me, called me a stupid woman, and sometimes he became violent.

## Chapter Eight

There was a time when my Norwegian sweetheart, Helge, to whom I'd been engaged, got in touch with me. He was visiting New York on business and wanted to get together for a drink for old time's sake. There was nothing more than that. He was married and I was married. He called and gave me his phone number. As I started writing it down on the blackboard in our kitchen, Mario appeared from around the corner with a look of rage on his face that terrified me. He must have heard the conversation. I tried to erase the number but I wasn't fast enough.

Mario hit me across the head so hard I saw stars. Amazingly, there was no visible injury, but, years later, I was told that when he was working in Italy the police there taught him how to hurt someone without leaving any marks. This was my life. I lived in fear that saying the wrong thing would set him off. The one blessing that came out of all this was my son, Joe. I definitely made the right decision in bringing him into this world. In spite of everything, I stayed in the marriage because of him.

The house was great for entertaining, especially for hosting my relatives from Norway who came to stay for a few weeks at a time. First and foremost was Mamma. She was quite a character and always good fun. On one of her visits we invited another couple, longtime friends, over for dinner. We were eating and laughing and forgetting to translate for Mamma, who didn't speak any English at all. But that didn't bother her. She turned to me and said, "You are all having such a good time. I've decided that every time you laugh, I will laugh, too."

One of the stories I love about Mamma involves the time she organized trips for a group of women on a cruise ship from Oslo to Copenhagen basically so she could get a free ticket. On the way back into Norway, going through customs, she was smuggling some alcohol to avoid paying tax. My Uncle Kaare, who was married to my mom's sister, my Aunt Eva, picked her up and wanted to know why she was walking in a funny manner. It turned out that a flask of booze had fallen down her pantyhose and she was working hard to make sure it didn't crash to the ground. Luckily, in spite of her awkward gait, she made it through without getting caught. Mamma was a constant source of humor—in contrast to my mother.

### Lillemor vs. Mario

Over the years, family members often visited us and sometimes we made the journey to Norway. It didn't matter whether we went there or they came to us, Mario stirred up trouble. When he was with my family, he always found something to fight about, yet I had to religiously spend Sundays and holidays with his family and was expected to be the perfect thankful guest.

As I mentioned, Lillemor and Mario had a stormy relationship. She told me she did not like a man who smiled when he was angry, and Mario often called her names. His mistreatment of me was bad enough, but it hurt me the most when he verbally abused my mother—even though I had my own issues with her—and there was nothing I could do to stop him. He was just a hateful, mean-spirited

## Chapter Eight

man who didn't attempt to hide his feelings toward me and my family.

The first time I tried to get a break from him, my escape was to go back to Norway—by myself. Soon into the vacation, however, something happened that would become typical of future visits. Lillemor wanted to control my time. She didn't want me to hang out with other family members; she just wanted me to spend time with her. For the last night of this trip I accepted a dinner invitation from Tante Eva and, as I was getting ready to leave, Odd told me Lillemor was in the bathroom—sobbing. It would be heartless of me to leave her alone on my last evening, he said. How could I hurt her so much?

They put unbearable pressure on me. I had no choice but to call Tante Eva and cancel. Now Tante Eva was mad at me. She was so upset that, when I got back to the States, she returned a gift I had given her of some beautiful bed sheets. That was a real slap in the face. I should not have let Lillemor manipulate me. I should have just walked out the door and gone for dinner with Tante Eva. There was something wrong with me. I took abuse from Mario and abuse from her and didn't fight back.

When Joe was about four or five, I took him on a trip to Norway without Mario. I don't know what Mario's problem was, but he became extremely belligerent when he couldn't immediately get hold of me when he phoned. What? He expected me to do nothing but sit by the phone waiting for his call? When we did connect, he lashed out, calling me all sorts of ugly names. Within forty-eight hours he was on a plane to join us. He couldn't stand the thought that I was out and about in Norway having a wonderful time without him.

I did not go completely mad because of my love for Joe, who was a pleasure from the day he was born. I had never experienced the benefit of my mother as a good role model, either as a child or as an adult, but I guess a basic nurturing instinct emerged in me. My whole life revolved around Joe. He meant everything to me.

Luckily, one thing Mario was not jealous of was my incredibly close relationship with my son. While I'm sure he only wanted the best for Joe, Mario was too concerned with the business to get much involved in Joe's life, even missing most of his sports activities.

When Joe was in fifth grade, I got the idea that I wanted him to go to a private school. I'd overheard other parents talking about which teachers were good and which ones weren't and—to my dismay and shame—it made me realize I had little real understanding of the American school system. A friend of Joe's told him that when he'd got bad grades his parents sent him to King School, a private school in Stamford, Connecticut, and that when he returned to public school he was ahead of the other students. I thought that sending Joe to the same school was an excellent idea, and Mario agreed.

I have no doubt it was one of the best decisions we ever made, although it was tough for Joe at the beginning. The first year there, he was unhappy and angry at me for making him switch schools. He also needed tutoring in

## Chapter Eight

English. That was no great surprise as he had an Italian-speaking father and a Norwegian-speaking mother. English was very much a second language for both of us. The kind, good-natured kid became difficult to deal with for a while, but it got better and, when he became a senior, he was elected president of the student body.

During these years, some of the best times were when Mamma came to stay. During one of her visits, I needed to pick up Joe from school because he had missed the school bus. I couldn't take her with me because I drove a two-seater. Mamma was worried.

She asked me what she would do if a big scary stranger came to the door. I assured her that no one would come to the house and she was perfectly safe, but she wasn't satisfied.

"At least give me the phone number for the police station," she said.

I had to laugh, "But, Mamma, what are you going to say? You don't speak English. They won't understand you."

"What?" she said, horrified. "The police don't speak Norwegian?"

Another day, the moment I arrived home from work, she ran down the stairs in a panic and said, "I told on Joe and now I've been punished."

She'd reported Joe to us for some misdemeanor he'd committed—I can't even remember what it was. Her punishment? A picture of Jesus that had been hanging in the guest room had vanished. She took it as a sign of some kind. Mario and I had received the picture as a wedding gift. It had a fancy frame made of shells. Let's say it was very ornate. I'd forgotten it was there until I suddenly noticed it one day when I passed by her room. Knowing how Mamma felt about Catholicism, I thought she'd prefer if it wasn't hanging in her room. So, I took it down and put it away in a closet. Mamma, however, was convinced that God was punishing her by making Jesus vanish from her bedroom.

I loved having her come to stay with us. Every night she'd go to bed with one of the books from a three-volume edition of *Gone with the Wind* tucked under her arm. When I went to bed some time later, I always checked in on her and every night it was the same sight: she was sitting upright, fast asleep, book folded over her chest, glasses down on her nose. On the nightstand was a sleeping pill. She never took it—having it there it just gave her a sense of security in case she needed help sleeping. A creature of habit.

Years later, when she was eighty-four, she came over with my two aunts. As the plane circled JFK airport, she looked out at the bright lights of New York, turned to Eva, and said, "Let's do this again real soon." She was planning another trip before she'd even arrived for this one. She'd crossed the Atlantic, a flight that's tiring for everyone, and was raring to go. Except there was one delay. I was waiting to meet them at the airport and my aunt had said she'd get Mamma a wheelchair. But there was no sign of them. I waited and waited until finally they appeared—the last people to get off the plane. No wheelchair.

"What happened to the wheelchair?" I demanded.

## Chapter Eight

"Oh, no," said my grandmother. "If God sees me in a wheelchair, he'll put me there permanently." That was Mamma.

Mamma loved Joe. And I'm so glad she got to see him mature into a fine young man. The years he attended King School set him up for the rest of his life and helped him become the man he is today. The trust he enjoyed from his peers and the confidence that grew inside of him figured into his success. It took a few years of hard work, but the reward was securing a place at a better college than if he'd stayed at public school. It helped, of course, that he was a handsome, well-mannered boy; sociable and gregarious. When Joe graduated from King School, he went to Richmond College, at the University of Richmond in Virginia, a beautiful old school dating back to 1840 whose campus includes a scenic lake and gardens.

While he was there, Joe met and fell in love with Trudy, a very pretty brunette with big green eyes. Not long after college they married and, while Joe's career took off, Trudy had her hands full with three growing boys. Unfortunately, Joe and Trudy grew apart and divorced after ten years. The blessing is that they gave me three wonderful and successful grandsons: Michael, who was hired by a leading financial institution after he graduated from a Philadelphia area college; Joey, who played professional soccer in Australia for a year after graduating from a Boston college; and Christian, who is studying engineering in Michigan. Joe became the father to them that his father never was to him.

# Chapter Nine

Around June 1974, we heard that Odd had died. Apparently, he had rented a rowing boat and, by himself, rowed out on the Oslo Fjord. The boat was later found empty and Odd's body was never found. Odd didn't know how to swim, so did he have too much to drink and fell into the water? Or did he take his own life by jumping in the cold waters of the fjord? To this day no one knows.

I can't pretend his death was a great loss. I had never cared for Odd. He was a strange, bitter man who ruined his life through drink. Lillemor, who wrote to tell me about his presumed death, had also long lost any feelings she might have had for him. They had got divorced some time before, and Odd had sneakily removed things from their apartment right under her nose. According to Tante Eva, he'd once told Lillemor she could jump off the balcony for all he cared. It had always been a tumultuous relationship

## Chapter Nine

and it had driven me out of Norway.

The last time Lillemor had seen Odd was at the divorce lawyer's office when he showed up blind drunk and fell asleep in the chair. The last time I'd seen him was when he had visited us in Connecticut with her several years earlier. They had already decided to divorce and had moved into separate apartments, so I never really understood why she brought him to the States, but the visit was a disaster. One day he sat at my kitchen table and, for some strange reason, insisted that more Germans were alive in Berlin after World War II than before. He was rambling. He didn't make any sense. Another day, I caught him in the kitchen guzzling vodka straight from the bottle. I told him that he was only hurting himself, "Odd, this is no way to live." All I got in response was a look of contempt. He was beyond the point of caring about anyone else's opinion (especially mine), or caring for himself.

One weekend not long after Lillemor and Odd returned to Norway, Mario, Joe, and I went up to Vermont for a break. On the way home, Mario was behind the wheel and, so that he wouldn't miss the entrance to the parkway, slammed on the brakes so suddenly that a large truck could not avoid ramming into the back of our car. Unfortunately for me, I had made the mistake of not wearing a seatbelt and was thrown around. The right side of my face was badly bruised, and I had to be taken to hospital to get stitches in the back of my head but I was the only one hurt, thank God.

No sooner did we get home than the phone rang—a routine call from Tante Eva. So, I related what happened.

"Shall I tell Lillemor?" she asked.

"Sure," I replied.

Lillemor didn't call. I never heard a word from her. Months later, I asked her why she hadn't bothered to check on us after she knew about the accident. Her response: "Because you told Eva first."

She was mad that her sister was aware of the accident before she was—as if that were a big deal. And, anyway, telling Eva first wasn't something I'd done deliberately. It took me a long time to realize how Lillemor had been manipulating me, and it took a family event in Norway for things to come to a head. Tante Berit and her family had moved back to Norway about ten years earlier and we got an invitation to attend her son's confirmation. Lillemor told me she was not going, and didn't want me to go, either. She made it sound like it would create a crisis.

Why didn't she want to attend? By this stage, she really didn't have much to do with the rest of the family. She knew Eva and Mamma would be there, and didn't want to handle that kind of interaction. Then there was the issue that Berit lived in a million-dollar home in one of Oslo's best neighborhoods. Lillemor probably didn't want to go "high society." She didn't want to dress up and be forced to be on her best behavior. She'd rather languish at home and let her new husband, a wonderful man called Fred Amundsen, take care of her.

When I told Tante Eva that Mario, Joe, and I probably should avoid the event because it would upset Lillemor it was the last straw for her. She let me have it.

"You are thirty-five years old. It's about time you took

## Chapter Nine

charge of your own life and start thinking for yourself," she fumed.

I knew she was right. Despite Lillemor's attitude, we went to Norway and had a wonderful time. We didn't visit Lillemor on that trip and never talked to her about it. It was a pivotal moment in our relationship. I'd put my foot down with my mother; it was going to be a lot longer before I could do the same with my husband.

Years later, I went back to Norway and decided not to tell Lillemor that I was in the country. I'd had enough. I just couldn't be in her company. We butted heads so much, it would ruin my visit there. I stayed with Tante Eva, who threw a cocktail party one night. Among the people at the party was Eva's best friend and, even though this woman didn't know my mother, she went out of her way to call her and reveal that her daughter was "secretly" in the country! Why this woman would go out of her way to do such a mean thing baffles me. That didn't do anything to help the already soured mother-daughter relationship.

# Chapter Ten

I'd become more and more involved in the business and was the pivotal liaison between Mario and the professionals like lawyers, accountants, and insurance brokers whose services we needed. Because, even though I say so myself, I was a good cook, I hosted large parties for business partners and friends. In many ways, I was the perfect wife. But our relationship was poisonous.

One day I was driving home in my treasured Porsche and it all got to me. Lillemor had told me never to cry, but I broke down in tears. (Yes, it is possible to cry in a Porsche!) I wasn't far from the house but the thought of going home to this man just sickened me. What the hell was I doing? I had to pull over to the side of the road until I could control my sobbing.

One morning when Joe was sixteen, he came downstairs and found me sitting on the living-room floor crying

## Chapter Ten

my heart out. My marriage was miserable and I needed to break away. I felt that I needed to get far, far away from Mario, but I couldn't live without Joe.

"Would you come live with me in Norway?" I asked him.

Joe replied, "Yes, Mom. But I'd want to come back to go to college in America."

His honest response made me realize there was no future for us in Norway. In my desperation to escape an abusive husband, I was proposing to go back to Norway and the mother and stepfather from whom I'd fled. What was I thinking? How could we do that? If I lived in Norway, and Joe went to college in the States, I could lose him forever.

It was around this time that another major incident occurred when Mario and I were invited for dinner at my girlfriend Wenche's house. She'd separated from her husband and was living with a new guy called Fred. When we arrived at their home, Fred gave me a big bear hug of a welcome. That didn't go down well with Mario whose jealousy knew no bounds. In a flash, his face darkened and I could tell he was struggling to control an angry outburst. It put me on guard. I knew all too well what the jealousy demon could do to Mario. All night long I watched every word I spoke and made a point of being cool toward Fred, who'd done nothing more than be friendly. It wasn't enough.

We drove home in silence. You could cut the atmosphere with a knife. That simple hug from Fred incensed Mario. Rage had been simmering inside him all evening as we ate dinner and engaged in seemingly cordial conversation. I

— 63

stared out the car window and didn't see it coming. Mario struck me viciously in the face with his clenched fist. As I doubled over in pain, he grabbed my hair and banged my head into the car window. I was hurt, but I was more shocked than anything else and sat there shaking. He never uttered a word. He kept his eyes firmly on the road and kept driving. When we stopped at an intersection, I threw open the car door and jumped out. Even though I was in high heels, I started walking home, away from the car, away from this crazy man. Mario desperately tried to get me back into the car.

"Get in, get in!" he yelled.

I refused and he took off.

I walked for miles alone along dark country roads, angry and hurt at my predicament yet determined to get home under my own steam. At one point, a police car stopped and the officers asked if I needed help. Without thinking, I reflexively replied I was all right. How stupid. I should have told them what happened. Keeping silent that night is one thing I will regret for the rest of my life.

The next day I called Wenche and told her how Mario had assaulted me. I asked if I had done or said anything that could have provoked the attack. I got her to ask Fred, too. Their response: "You did not do anything wrong, Venke. What Mario did was abuse. No woman should be treated like that." They were shocked and sought to comfort me.

I'd never told anyone, not even Wenche, who was a really close friend, about the verbal and physical abuse. It was the kind of thing you didn't talk about; it stayed inside the marital home. Mario got very upset that day when I told him I'd seriously considered revealing his assault to the police. He said, if I turned him in it would hurt his business! That's what he really cared about—negative publicity would hurt his business. Our marriage was secondary.

To make amends, Mario bought two first class tickets for a vacation on the Norwegian Cruise Line, sailing the Mediterranean and stopping at ports like Monte Carlo, St. Tropez, and Sardinia. We sailed on a small luxury ship that carried only a hundred passengers and, each night, he insisted I call room service and order caviar. Mario was on his best behavior and it was the finest vacation I ever had. Before we left for the cruise, I gave him an ultimatum: we could not carry on living like this. I would file for divorce if he did not see a psychiatrist, something he agreed to do.

I didn't know this was the classic pattern in an abusive relationship. The woman is brutalized. The man begs forgiveness. He makes amends. He shows his good side. The woman forgives him. And then the dark side reappears. The cycle continues.

## Fight for Independence

Mario found a psychiatrist, Dr. John A. Larson, born in the U.S. to a Norwegian mother and Swedish father. A towering figure of a man, almost seven feet tall, and in his sixties, his face was etched with the grief he'd suffered when his son was killed in a gruesome accident while vacationing in England. Somehow his son was dragged under a train after his backpack became snagged.

After a few sessions with Mario, Dr. Larson suggested I attend one of them. I did, thinking it would be time well spent if it could help Mario understand what caused his abusive behavior and put a stop to it. But I came away confused. It seemed like I was being put on the defensive. The doctor wanted to know: Why did I wear such short skirts? Why did I wear high heels? I asked myself, was he suggesting it was my fault Mario behaved as he did? I was the one who had demanded Mario get help for his jealousy and anger. Was everything now being blamed on me? This was not what Mario needed. Mario was insanely jealous, no matter what I wore, or how I behaved. I should have challenged Dr. Larson but I didn't.

I'd planned a getaway with a couple of girlfriends to a small condo we owned in the Vermont ski resort of Sugarbrush, but, at the last minute, my friends couldn't make it and Mario insisted he come instead. Great. It was Mario I needed to get a break from, but I decided not to protest.

I regretted it almost as soon as we hit the road. During the four-hour drive, he kept up a non-stop barrage of criticism. He found fault with everything about me. By the time we got to our Sugarbrush condo, I was worn out. As I walked into the kitchen, I heard his voice behind me.

"I see you have the same mess here that we have at home."

"What mess, Mario?"

"There," he said, pointing at a pile of papers, some envelopes and newspapers, lying on the kitchen counter.

Without a word, I picked up the pile and threw everything into the air.

## Chapter Ten

"Now, it's a mess, Mario."

I took my skis and marched out into the snow. In the restaurant at the top of the mountain, I bought a can of beer but my hands shook so much I couldn't open it. I refused to talk to Mario the rest of the weekend. On the way home, he suggested that maybe I should also see Dr. Larson by myself. I could not have agreed more. I recognized that I needed help to figure out my life.

I wanted to try and understand why our marriage had spiraled out of control. I was alarmed about Mario's increasingly jealous and aggressive behavior, but I knew I had issues of my own stemming from my upbringing in Norway. It made sense to get some counseling from Dr. Larson.

I visited Dr. Larson twice a week, while Mario stopped going and never went back. Every time I sat in the waiting room, my stomach was tied up in knots as I anticipated my session. I talked frankly and revealed to Dr. Larson all the painful and embarrassing episodes in my life, especially my strained relationship with Lillemor and her bizarre marriage to Odd and how, as I'd gotten older, I'd bounced from an abusive relationship with my mother and her husband to an abusive relationship with my husband. I revealed what I'd discovered about my father. Most of all, it seemed my struggles were with all the unanswered questions I had about events Lillemor had never fully explained. So much of my early life was shrouded in mystery.

Dr. Larson's office was a refuge where I could be myself, even if discussing the ravages and pitfalls of my life frequently brought me to tears. Dr. Larson described those tears as a cleansing process. He seemed like a father figure to me. Mario saw it differently. He even became jealous of the time I spent with Dr. Larson and suggested that, instead of individual counseling, we see him together. Neither I nor Dr. Larson thought that was a good idea.

There was one particular story I told the doctor that led to a moment of revelation I hadn't expected. Joe had started college in Richmond, Virginia, and Mario and I went to visit him. The three of us were sitting together at a small table in our hotel's bar. As usual, we talked about the business and, as I gave my opinion about an issue, Mario interrupted, "What do you know about business? You're just a stupid woman." Joe turned to his father and spoke up in my defense, "That was uncalled for, Dad, and if you ever talk to me that way when I start working for you, I will not be there very long."

I was glad he had the courage to stand up to his dad, even if I didn't.

Of course, I couldn't wait to tell Dr. Larson all about the latest example of Mario's boorishness, expecting a sympathetic response. Instead, he said, "Tell me something, Venke. Why is it OK for your son to speak up, but it's not OK for you?" I had all sorts of excuses: I had not wanted to make a scene; I didn't want it to be uncomfortable for Joe; and so on. The truth was, I did not know how to make a verbal stand in my defense. And that was the moment when I realized what had been wrong for so long.

Little by little, I began to speak up for myself. I would say, "Do not talk to me like that, Mario. Do not call me names, Mario." The assertiveness had the desired effect. Mario became quiet when I wouldn't let him get away with his verbal attacks. It made me stronger, and it made him more insecure. I'd kept silent for too many years of my marriage. I'd passively accepted the abuse without speaking up in defense of myself. Like many victims I did what I could to avoid being hurt again. I was fearful of confrontations. I was not being me.

I strove to become independent. I did things I'd always wanted to do. I took private flying lessons in a two-seater Cessna, although I have to admit when it came to lesson eight and the booklet said I would have to stall the plane, I decided I'd had enough of flying! I attended a Dale Carnegie course and overcame my fear of public speaking. Fear doesn't cover it. I was terrified. I was someone who was scared to stand up at a house party and play charades but who, in time, became so confident and loved performing so much, that it was hard to get me down from the "stage." That was a nice accomplishment. After twenty years, I also quit smoking a pack a day of my favorite Dunhill cigarettes. I had a newfound confidence. I was determined to feel good about myself.

# Chapter Eleven

One day in the winter of 1986, I was sitting across from Dr. Larson when he gave me a particularly serious and thoughtful look. He pursed his lips, and I could tell he was weighing his words carefully. He told me, "Venke, you will never really feel good about yourself until you find out something good about your father." He went on, "It could be something from his childhood, something about his education, anything, just as long as it is something positive."

This was a stunning observation. What could I do? What might I find out? Did I really want to know more than I did? I'd always had the feeling that Lillemor was holding back, that there was a part of her life (and mine) that she did not want to delve into, for whatever reason.

But this was *my* life. Surely, I deserved to know more about my parentage? Something had been nagging at me for years. Maybe now was the time to confront it, to

CHAPTER ELEVEN

stop being passive and, with my new confidence, to try to unravel the family history?

I'd often wondered about Lillemor's revelation that I had a half-brother in Germany whom, she predicted, I would meet one day. But she'd never elaborated, and we'd never discussed it. Lillemor was a forbidding presence, while I was introverted, quiet and withdrawn. I never dared question her. It might seem strange, but it was the way she'd molded me during my earliest formative years.

Perhaps I could connect with my father's family in Germany? They were my relatives, after all, and they'd been hidden from me. How could I track them down after so many years had passed? If I found them, would they want to know me? Why would they? They'd probably refuse to have anything to do with me. These thoughts rattled through my head and I agonized over the right thing to do. I could not let go of the idea. I made the decision: I was going to search for them, and I wouldn't stop until I found them. It was a sense of determination I'd never had before.

**BEGINNING THE SEARCH**

I began by visiting the German Consulate in New York. Heinrich Fehlis was a prominent man. They must be able to locate his records and give me something about his background. Or, so I thought. But the people at the consulate made it very clear they had absolutely no interest in helping me. They didn't just give me the cold shoulder; they gave me the frigidly cold shoulder. They were rude and dismissive. I was shocked and disappointed and I had to accept that this avenue was a dead end. Their attitude should have made me suspicious. It didn't. But it did make me more determined to keep looking.

Fortunately, my friend Wenche, whose ex-husband Richard was German, put me in touch with an older German couple who kindly agreed to help. The husband's sister lived in Germany and worked for the police. With the kind of database available to her, she could probably track down my half-brother—if he existed. The only snag was that she needed to know where my father had grown up. I had no idea. I had no option other than to ask Lillemor and that would expose to her what I was doing.

I phoned my mother in Norway. It was not a friendly conversation. "Lillemor, where was my father born?"

"Why do you want to know? What good can come of it? Just leave things be," she snapped, and refused to tell me.

I persisted. I insisted. The conversation got quite heated. And then she caved in. My father had been raised in an industrial town called Wuppertal in North Rhine-Westphalia, east of the major city of Düsseldorf and south of the Ruhr area. It is the town where Aspirin was developed, where philosopher Friedrich Engels, who wrote *The Communist Manifesto* with Karl Marx, had lived, and where people had died in one of the first Nazi concentration camps.

Our German contacts went to work. Within a month or so, in March 1986, I got the answer. One of my father's cousins still lived in Wuppertal and he'd told them that I did have a half-brother whose name was Peter Fehlis and that he lived in Aachen. And there was more. The German

## Chapter Eleven

woman had spoken with Peter, and, not only was he aware I was searching for him, he'd also agreed she could give me his phone number.

My half-brother was for real. He was alive. His name was Peter. And now I had his phone number. He was just a few digits away.

As impulsive as ever, I didn't waste a second thinking about it. Sitting on my bed I grabbed the phone and, with trembling hands, dialed. I hadn't rehearsed what I was going to say, even though I'd dreamed about this moment so many times. The phone rang and rang. I was so nervous I almost hung up. Then a male voice answered. It was Peter.

"Hi, Peter. I am your half-sister Venke from Norway."

And without pausing for breath I asked, "Would you like to meet with me?"

Without any hesitation, he said, "Hello, Venke. Yes, of course I will meet with you."

He had a kind voice. He was warm and receptive. It was beyond belief.

I told him I would call him back just as soon as I'd booked my ticket. I put down the phone and cried for a long time. I cried for joy. I cried for relief. An upsurge of emotions buried for so many years wracked my body and my mind. The feeling I had when I heard Peter's voice is indescribable. I was forty-one years old and I was going to meet my half-brother and my other family for the first time. They'd lived their lives; I'd lived my life. We knew nothing about one another. It was simply wonderful to make this connection after all these years.

However, there was Mario; always Mario. He'd been in the room when I made the call. I had absolutely no desire for him to travel with me to Germany for this momentous meeting. In all the time we'd been together, he'd done nothing but badmouth my mother and my father and the German race in general.

I made it clear I wanted to go by myself, but there was no way he was going to miss out. In spite of all the nasty things he'd said about the Germans over the years, he was coming no matter what. Even though he was on crutches following a skiing accident, he was determined to make the trip. He had to get his nose into everything. In his usual bombastic manner, Mario took control and went right ahead and booked airline tickets and hotel rooms for a week-long visit to Aachen. Within a week we were on our way.

# Chapter Twelve

The flight across the Atlantic from JFK to Aachen gave me plenty of time to think. What would Peter be like? Would he resemble our father? How lucky was I that Peter had been so open and willing to meet me? Had he known about me all these years? Had he ever dreamed of us getting together? What would he and other members of my German family be able to tell me about my father? There was so much I didn't know. I'd never felt completely whole. Would this connection help fill the emptiness I'd endured for so long?

I barely slept on the overnight flight. I cried quietly a lot of the time as I went through a bewildering rollercoaster of emotions. Mario's presence irritated me, especially when we landed in Germany and he hobbled off the plane on his crutches leaving me to handle our carry-on bags. Why couldn't he have just stayed at home? This was nothing to do with him. Why had he muscled in on one of the most momentous events of my life?

My irritation quickly vanished when we passed through customs and immigration and I spotted a smiling face beaming at me from behind a fence. It was Peter. We instantly recognized each other. As we worked our way through the crowd of people in the arrivals hall, Peter, his wife, and their two children stepped forward to warmly greet us. They literally welcomed us with open arms and I couldn't have been more thrilled.

No sooner had we entered Peter's home than the doorbell rang and there stood a distinguished-looking man and a younger woman bearing a huge bouquet of beautiful flowers. To my astonishment it turned out to be my father's youngest brother, Ingolf, and his daughter, Ingeborg. I didn't even know Ingolf and Ingeborg existed, yet they'd shown up to meet me. I brazenly stared at Ingolf and thought, this is how my father would look if he were still alive. Ingeborg was a beautiful woman, two years my senior. It was overwhelming. Not only had I found a half-brother after all these years, but I'd also found an uncle and a cousin.

They made a huge fuss over me, and immediately took me in as one of the family. I had so many questions for them; they had so many questions for me. It was a joyous, jumbled conversation as we tripped over each other's words getting acquainted and sharing our life stories. I couldn't speak German and they didn't speak Norwegian but thankfully we had English as a common language.

# Chapter Twelve

They were truly interested in me and what I'd done with my life. I felt safe and whole, perhaps for the first time ever. There was no pretense. There was no secrecy. It was a wonderful feeling. And for once Mario didn't insult or embarrass me. Why had I waited until I was forty-one to seek them out? When I returned to our hotel that first night after spending these precious hours with Peter and his family, I couldn't help myself. The tears kept coming. They were tears of joy, in many ways, but something else, something difficult to explain. It was as if every time I cried, some of the pain inside of me became a little easier to bear.

Another night Mario and I decided to have a nightcap in the bar, which sat in the middle of the foyer of the very old, elegant hotel where we were staying. The bar was virtually empty. Two men came in and one of them, a tall, heavyset, blond guy sat next to me, took out a cigar and started to light it up. The bartender stepped over and politely informed him that smoking was not allowed.

"There's nobody here," said this man, waving his arm to indicate the almost-empty bar. "Nobody cares."

"I do," I declared instantly.

And that shut him down. There was something about him that made my skin crawl, something I detested. It wasn't just his arrogant attitude about smoking. I looked at him and wondered, were you one of those soldiers who tortured people? Meanwhile, the bartender disappeared laughing behind a column, grateful that I'd spoken up and supported him. This was the new Venke. The old Venke would not have taken a stance.

### THE SHOCKING REVELATION

Aachen sits in the corner of Germany nestled close to the borders of both Belgium and the Netherlands. It is a city steeped in history. The Romans nursed their war wounds and stiff joints in the hot, soothing waters of the town's famed mineral springs. In the year 974, Emperor Charlemagne, the first Holy Roman Emperor, proclaimed it to be the capital of his vast Frankish Empire. The magnificent Aachener Dom (Aachen Cathedral), where Charlemagne is buried and where more than thirty German kings were crowned, is the country's first UNESCO World Heritage site.

Aachen is a city of beautiful medieval buildings and cute outdoor cafes where you can sample its most famous delicacy, Aachener Printen, a spicy Lebkuchen pastry similar to gingerbread. To me it was a city where a dream had been realized, where, after four decades, I'd met the half-brother I'd never known. History, distance, and family dysfunction had kept us apart, but now we were together, and making up for lost time.

On our second day there, a Sunday, Mario and I were invited to a family dinner at Ingeborg's home in Cologne, about an hour and a half away. When we got there, before the meal, we all went for a stroll along the banks of the River Rhine, one of the great rivers of Europe. It was a beautiful day. I reveled in the feeling of family, of belonging. Apart from giving birth to Joe, this experience was undoubtedly the highlight of my life. I had not imagined it could turn out so well. Peter and the family could easily have rejected

CHAPTER TWELVE

me. They could have refused any kind of contact. Instead, they'd wrapped their arms around me.

As we walked along the Rhine, admiring the view and enjoying the Sunday afternoon tranquility, I felt something bump against my leg. I looked down and realized Uncle Ingolf was surreptitiously tapping me with a rolled-up newspaper. It looked old—faded and slightly curled. Puzzled, I looked at it him and he nodded his head, silently encouraging me to take it from him. It was odd, furtive behavior, but he obviously didn't want the others to see what he was doing. So, I took the paper and stashed it in my handbag.

Back at Ingeborg's home, which doubled as her beautiful antiques store, my curiosity got the better of me and I quickly retrieved the newspaper out of my bag. It was *Expressen*, a major Swedish paper and was published in March, 1969. I sat down at a table to read it, joined by Ingeborg and Peter. There was a large photo of my father in uniform and one of the headlines blared,

"Fiancée of the Butcher of Norway Smuggled Out to Sweden."

In this sensationalized account, Heinrich Fehlis was also described as the "Desk Executioner." While he might not have pulled the trigger, he signed the death warrants of many. He had not been an officer in the Wehrmacht, the regular German Army, as I'd assumed, or been led to believe. He was the chief of Gestapo, the most ruthless and reviled of all the Nazis. When he failed to escape at the end of the war, he committed suicide. And apparently, to

— 79

add to my horror, my mother had later tried to kill herself, and had been committed to a mental hospital.

All this, and much more, was there in black and white. My heart thumped harder and harder as I read paragraph after paragraph in the pages of *Expressen*. The information had been held in classified documents and kept secret for twenty-four years. There was revelation after revelation, detail after detail, that I discovered for the first time. I had no idea. No one had mentioned anything to me. The article that Lillemor had shared with me from a Norwegian newspaper on her visit to the States years earlier didn't contain such excruciating details and had been written in a more matter-of-fact style. It wasn't sensationalized. I remembered, though, I'd thought it strange at the time that parts of that article had been cut out. Those parts were the description of my father as the chief of Gestapo.

The Swedish newspaper only identified my mother by her first names Else Johanne and referred to her as the beautiful Norwegian mistress of the German Gestapo chief. She'd lived in Sweden, it claimed, under a cover name. It wasn't a cover name at all—everyone just knew her as "Lillemor." I already knew something of the "horse trade"—the bartering for the safety of Lillemor and me in return for the safety of thousands of prisoners. That part of the story had been highlighted in the Norwegian newspaper article. Now it began to make more sense. The Allies and Sweden were fearful that the end of the war might provoke a bloodbath in which the defeated Germans and their Norwegian collaborators slaughtered their prisoners.

## Chapter Thirteen

The *Expressen* article provided new and important details about the secret negotiations between Fehlis and Harry Söderman, who'd overseen the military training in Sweden of twelve thousand Norwegians. Both men had their own agendas. As reported earlier, Fehlis and Söderman, had met a few times, most notably on April 22,1945, on the Swedish-Norwegian border. During that meeting, they discussed Söderman's demand that all the Gestapo's political prisoners—more than five thousand—be transferred to Sweden.

On May 5, Fehlis and Söderman talked by phone. Although Heinrich Himmler the Third Reich's overall Gestapo chief, one of the most powerful men in Nazi Germany and one of the architects of the Holocaust, had not responded to Söderman's demand, Fehlis encouraged Söderman to travel to Oslo to continue negotiations in person.

On May 7, the newly trained members of the Norwegian Liberation Army stood on the Swedish side of the border, ready to march into their homeland if any of the Nazi forces refused to obey the capitulation order. It was a tense, nerve-wracking time, a potentially explosive situation.

In the early hours of the following morning, Söderman, now settled into the Oslo police chief's office, received a strange phone call from Fehlis requesting an urgent meeting. The Norwegian Resistance suspected an ambush and were not enthusiastic. But it was agreed that Fehlis's car would be allowed to drive into an area behind the remand prison.

In his book, *Skandinaviskt Mellanspel* (*Scandinavian Interlude*), Söderman wrote, somewhat evasively, that Fehlis wanted, "a purely private conversation." The two men paced backwards and forwards for the best part of an hour under the watchful eye of men whose machine guns were trained on their every move. Fehlis sought to position himself favorably and reiterated that there would be no resistance from his men and emphasized he had contributed to a peaceful dismantling of German power in Oslo by keeping a promise for the prisoners' safe release. He also said that instead of pursuing a plan to go underground, all members of the Gestapo would stay in place and face the consequences. Wrote Söderman, "Then he entered his car and left. I would never seem him alive again."

Through Fehlis's cooperation, Söderman took command of the Grini concentration camp, where five thousand prisoners were held, and he also secured the freedom of five hundred prisoners in Oslo jails, some of whom

## Chapter Thirteen

had been sentenced to death. The Germans surrendered without incident.

After Fehlis departed, Söderman told his assistant, Captain Trofelt, that Fehlis wanted a favor in return for all the assistance he had already given.

It was Trofelt who told the *Expressen* newspaper: "He wanted Söderman in some way—he did not say how—to transport a certain lady, whom he called his wife, and whose name he mentioned, to Sweden.... Fehlis's child with the woman, was to accompany her."

Söderman was reluctant. If he agreed, and it ever came to light, the Norwegians would feel he had betrayed them because the woman, a collaborator with a high-level Nazi, would have escaped justice. Söderman was also nervous because he didn't know how he could pull it off, especially as the woman did not have a passport or visa. The solution he came up with was to personally escort the woman and child in a chauffeur-driven car provided by the Oslo police.

### Escape to Sweden

In the end, the border crossing was uneventful. Söderman and Trofelt flashed their Foreign Service couriers' passports and the guards didn't bother to look in the back of the car where Lillemor was crouched under a blanket with her three-month-old baby. Once in the safety of Sweden, the group stopped for coffee at the district police superintendent's home in the border town of Charlottenberg, before catching the night train to Stockholm. Söderman didn't explain the presence of the woman and child and the local police chief knew better than to question the celebrated Harry Söderman.

Trofelt described Lillemor as, "rather calm, very silent, not particularly interested in anything other than the baby . . . and very beautiful." Trofelt also claimed that Fehlis gave Söderman 20,000 Norwegian crowns to help Lillemor start a new life in Sweden. The notes, he claimed, were later discovered to be German forgeries—a statement that other accounts contradict.

The Swedish government documents that had been classified secret for so long revealed that at least until the late summer of 1945, Lillemor lived under a false name in the Söder district of Stockholm. According to the documents, as revealed by the newspaper, after she discovered that her lover had committed suicide, she unsuccessfully tried to kill herself. As a result, Söderman convinced her to sign an application to be admitted to Beckomberga Hospital, a psychiatric institution. While she had clear suicidal tendencies, the physicians recorded in their notes that she was not mentally ill.

According to them she did tell stories that were a mixture of truth and lies. She said she'd married a lawyer in Norway and lived with him until a catastrophe occurred and she moved to Sweden with her baby. She refused to talk about the catastrophe saying, "I do not want to say anything without asking Associate Professor Harry Söderman."

The doctors' impression of her was that she gave a clear and precise account, appeared self-possessed and composed, and intended to commit suicide as soon as she

## Chapter Thirteen

had an opportunity, as "it was the only way out."

The medical records, according to *Expressen*, showed that the suicidal thoughts gradually disappeared, but still Lillemor did not show any real zest for life. The desperation had turned into a strong, cool reserve. She was eager to get lipstick and other cosmetics so she could care for her appearance while in hospital. She talked about her "German husband who is dead" and it was obvious that she had been extremely fond of him. She also said that she had no intention of returning to Norway: "They would only put me in prison although I have never had any interest in politics."

The government files revealed other interesting snippets. Söderman kept in close contact with the hospital authorities until Lillemor was discharged in January 1946 without a diagnosis of mental illness ever being placed in her record. Lillemor was separated from her baby for a considerable time while hospitalized and, with her permission, a female relative (supposedly a paternal aunt) had taken the child back to Norway, according to the government files. The newspaper reported there was also a tantalizing reference to a man later revealed to be a Russian agent who "played a certain part."

Sitting at a highly polished antique table with Ingeborg and Peter either side of me, I was transported back in time. I never knew my father had been chief of the dreaded Gestapo. I knew enough of history to be aware that the Gestapo committed all kinds of atrocities in the name of the Third Reich. I never knew my father had killed himself or that my mother had tried to do the same. I never knew she had been admitted to a mental hospital.

Could this really all be true? I could ask Lillemor, but we didn't talk that much and her reaction when I'd asked for the name of Fehlis's home town had been downright hostile. And she had misled me all these years. I didn't for one second consider calling her. I called Tante Eva instead, knowing she would give me straight, honest answers while half-hoping she would tell me it was all nonsense. I couldn't wait another minute. So, I asked my hosts if I could call her. Tearfully, I got her on the line and poured out my discoveries.

"Yes, Venke. It is all true."

# Chapter Fourteen

The newspaper with its damning information about my father lay open on top of the table. My half-brother Peter and cousin Ingeborg sat on either side of me, comforting me. I was still in shock. They'd known the truth for most of their lives, but had wanted to break it to me gently. Unfortunately, Uncle Ingolf had beaten them to it. Why had he given me the newspaper so surreptitiously, I asked Peter, who just laughed, and said, "He is always so dramatic. That's uncle Ingolf. Don't worry about it."

Lillemor had kept this secret from me for forty-one years. She hadn't told me that the man she'd fallen in love with was a cold-blooded Hitler acolyte who'd routinely sent men to their deaths. What had her life been like? What had she gone through? I couldn't begin to imagine what she had experienced as the lover of a man at the highest levels of the Gestapo who was enforcing the occupation of her country. How despised she must have been for consorting with him and bearing his child.

I'd had enough of Lillemor's narcissistic, abusive, and drunken behavior. The revelation about my father's Nazi past was the ultimate betrayal. She'd only ever talked about my father in glowing terms and reminisced about the passion of their love affair. She'd painted a picture of a fairy-tale wartime romance that came to a tragic end. Why hadn't she been caring and honest enough to share the shattering information with me years earlier? Why hadn't she said something when I asked where Fehlis was born? She knew I was bound to unearth the truth once I tracked down my half-brother. Why did she let me continue my quest until I found out in the worst possible way—by reading a sensationalized newspaper story?

Peter and Ingeborg tried to ease the pain. It had not been easy for Peter, either. He told me a story from his own childhood. One day he'd shown kids at school a photograph of our father standing next to a famous German poet. But Fehlis was wearing his Nazi uniform in the photo. His so-called friends turned on Peter, and he was attacked and beaten day after day. In their young minds he was guilty of the sins of his father. It made me realize that a generation of younger Germans had suffered under the shame of the crimes committed by their parents' generation during World War II.

The newspaper headline also described my mother as Fehlis's fiancée. Had they got it right? Weren't my mother and father married? I'd always understood they were, despite occasional hints to the contrary. I told Peter and Ingeborg about the occasion in January 1965 when Lillemor had been

## Chapter Fourteen

so upset upon hearing a news report about a former Gestapo officer who had been captured and jailed more than twenty years after his crimes. She'd said the man, Hellmuth Reinhard, was a witness at their wedding. Would she have invented that? Peter didn't think they could have got married, because Fehlis was still married to his mother, whom he'd left behind in Germany. Ingeborg, though, believed a high-ranking Nazi could finagle the paperwork to do whatever he wanted. One newspaper account maintained that papers asking for permission to marry were on their way to Hitler for his signature, but he killed himself before they arrived. I had my doubts that a wedding had taken place, legal or not, and suspected Peter was right. Something else Lillemor had not been honest about.

I composed myself in time for dinner, but the atmosphere was charged with emotional undercurrents as everyone felt the enormity of the knowledge I'd acquired in such a strange way. Mario, though, was back to his usual thoughtless self, and embarrassed me at the dinner table by asking me to relate an incident when Joe was born.

"Venke, tell them how you felt your father was in the room with you," he announced.

I looked at him in horror and didn't say a word. It was true. I'd had a strange feeling that my father was reincarnated in my son, Joe. Dinner with my newfound family was not the place to talk about it, especially after what we'd just learned about my father's role in the Gestapo.

Mario persisted, urging me to relate the story, "Go on, Venke, tell them."

All I could do was bring myself to admit it was true.

After dinner, Ingeborg invited me to join her for a private conversation, and we went down a spiral staircase into her bedroom.

"I want you to know, Venke," she told me, "that our family does not believe in reincarnation. But since you told us what you experienced at Joe's birth, I have something to tell you."

When she was a young girl, Ingeborg had gone to a private school in Switzerland where she had many friends from different countries. Some years later, one of these friends, a Swedish girl, sent her the very same newspaper article Uncle Ingolf had handed me.

But what Ingeborg really wanted to talk about was life after death. She related a story about going on a summer vacation to Paris with a group of schoolfriends and their visit to a woman who was a spiritualist and medium. During the séance, the medium asked Ingeborg, "Do you know anyone named Heinrich?" Ingeborg said no, but when the medium insisted, she remembered she had heard of an uncle called Heinrich, an uncle she'd never met, who'd died in the war. Then the medium maintained, "He says that he does not like it where he is; he says he misses the family."

Where was he? If my father was a Nazi and the chief of Gestapo, most people would think it deserved to be Hell, but, when we got home, Mario went to see a psychic who told him that Fehlis was trapped in Purgatory. I don't believe in Hell or Purgatory, but I'd prefer he wasn't burning in Hell and I was glad Mario passed on that information. I was emotionally confused, but it gave me some measure of comfort.

## Chapter Fifteen

Knowing the truth about my father somehow empowered me. I continued to become stronger and more independent while, at the same time, my marriage continued to deteriorate. The stronger I grew, the more insecure Mario became. He was jealous of anything I did that didn't involve him, anything that showed I could take care of myself and have a life of my own.

He'd changed to a different psychiatrist, Dr. Wasserman, and then stopped seeing him. It was too painful, he told me. Instead, he found a woman in Greenwich, Connecticut, who channeled spirits. He believed in her probably because she told him exactly what he wanted to hear. Not surprisingly, a few years later, the authorities forced her out of business. Presumably, the spirits had not been able to warn her that she was about to be exposed as a fraud.

# Venke

With Joe at college, our home was empty. I no longer had any reason to pretend everything was OK between Mario and me, and the strain began to tell. One high spot in my life was a monthly get-together for dinner with seven other Norwegian women, alternating between one another's homes. It was an enjoyable culinary social event that lasted well into the night. Mario didn't like it, but there wasn't anything he could do about it.

## A Marriage Ends

It was one of these dinners in 1987 that precipitated the event that finally ended our marriage. Mario had slept in the guest room the night before, but came in to the bedroom to wake me around 6:00 a.m. I guess he was irritated because I'd had such a good time with my friends and he probably hadn't had much sleep. I hadn't got to bed until late and I was aggravated at being awakened so early, especially as I needed to be fresh for a flying lesson that morning.

"Venke, why am I so jealous of you?" he asked me, grabbing hold of my shoulder, gripping hard, and trying to turn me to face him.

I snapped, "Mario, you need help. Please go back to Dr. Wasserman."

I climbed out of bed, turned my back on him, and headed for the bathroom, not realizing how enraged he was. I didn't make it to the bathroom. He grabbed me around my neck, threw me to the floor, and started kicking me. I curled up into a ball until he'd vented his anger and stopped. Without a word, I straightened my pajamas, went

## Chapter Fifteen

downstairs, and sat in the living room while Mario stormed off to work. At precisely 9:00 a.m., I called a divorce attorney. At 12 noon, I was in his office. The marriage was over.

I showed the attorney the large black and blue marks that were already forming on my hip and detailed the sequence of events in our deteriorating marriage. The lawyer pulled no punches. He'd seen enough marital relationships fall apart in ugly ways. He told me a particularly gruesome story about a Danish airline stewardess whose husband had killed her and fed her body into a machine that turned logs into wood chips. Perhaps he was trying to scare me. If so, he succeeded.

As the days passed, I became increasingly nervous and agitated. We were living under the same roof and Mario was volatile. Was I in danger? I decided to talk to Dr. Larson, but he was on vacation. I asked Mario for permission to speak with Dr. Wasserman, and he agreed, but only if he came with me. Dr. Wasserman told Mario to take a seat in the waiting room while he talked with me. Inside the doctor's sanctuary, I spilled my guts, revealing my years of mental and physical suffering. Did Dr. Wasserman think I was in serious danger?

I was astonished when Dr. Wasserman went out and invited Mario to join us, whereupon he asked him: "Do you remember what you told me about the time you were a young boy and in love with a girl in Italy? One day she came around the corner and saw you pulling a cart full of scrap metal? Do you remember how embarrassed you were?"

He went on to talk about Mario's inferiority complex and how poorly he handled feeling humiliated. At one point, he looked at me, then at Mario, and declared, "She is fighting for her survival." He said it again. Turning to Mario, he said, "Stand up and say out loud, 'I'm sick.'" Mario, to my surprise, did as he was instructed. The two men hugged. And the session was over. As we walked down the corridor, Marco apologized, saying, "My God, what have I done to you all these years?"

That was what I needed to hear and, in the car on the way home, I took a conciliatory approach and assured him, "Mario, there is no need to tell anyone. This is just between you and me." I said I wouldn't even tell Joe. But Mario, it seemed, wanted to make a confession of his misdeeds and insisted he needed to call his mother and his brother, Lenny.

They arrived at our home soon after we did and I went upstairs to the bedroom, leaving them to talk. After a while Mario called for me to sit with them at the kitchen table. The back-pedaling began immediately: "You know, Venke, I have always treated you like a princess." I was not going along with it, this time.

"Really?" I said, pulling down the zipper of my slacks, revealing the darkening multicolored bruises on my hip to my mother-in-law and brother-in-law, "Is this the way to treat a princess?" There was silence.

"Lenny, I want him out," I told his brother, asking him to take Mario home with him. I did not want him under the same roof. Our marriage of twenty-one years was done.

## Chapter Fifteen

The next few weeks were a nightmare. Mario threatened to kill himself and he let the business go to hell. He called Joe at college every day, crying and complaining. I heard from friends that he was badmouthing me, blaming me for everything. I thought to myself: for years I've worked hard to be a good wife. I've fed him and his family, attended all their events, had parties for him and for the business. I listened to all his endless business talk. Hell, I worked for the business and made a major contribution. And this is the thanks I get?

In the end, I wrote to Dr. Wasserman asking him to get Mario to stop; Joe had enough challenges of his own to deal with and so did I. Not long afterward, I decided to tell my friend Turi what I'd discovered when I was in Germany, so we met for lunch in the restaurant at her private club. As I began to reveal the news, she put her hand over mine and said, "I know this, little friend." She always called me little friend, a term of endearment. I liked that. But how could she know? She knew because Mario had called at their home one evening and gleefully told them all about my Gestapo father! I couldn't believe he'd stooped so low.

The next day, as Joe was home on vacation, I told him what had happened. He was shocked. Mario had asked him for Turi and Leon's contact information, and had promised him he would not say anything about my father's past. For the first time since our return from Germany I began to cry. I felt betrayed. Mario had used our son and lied to him. Two weeks later, when Turi's mother was visiting from Norway, I invited the three of them to come over for dinner. I wondered if Leon would show up after Mario's revelations but he did, and he didn't raise the subject. He was a real gentleman.

Sometime later, Turi's mom, Mrs. Josefsen, became gravely ill and they called me to her bedside at their home. As I sat alongside her she held my hand tight and with deep concern asked me, "How will it go for you, now that you're getting divorced?" This wonderful woman was lying on her deathbed and all she cared about was how I would make it on my own. I was very touched. No wonder I loved her so. I had become deeply attached to her. She was like the mother I never had, and her passing was a time of deep sorrow.

### A New Identity

I was determined to make it on my own just fine. I'd been working my way toward full independence for a while. I could do it. In 1988 the divorce went through. Mario didn't want me to keep his last name. I definitely did not want to continue to be a Devivo: it would be too painful to go forward with my new life bearing that name. I insisted, however, on keeping the name while Joe was still in college so there was no confusion.

Who would I become? As a child I was Wenche (not Venke) Schaug, my mother's last name. And that's who I'd been when I met Mario. Should I revert to Schaug? I gave it a lot of thought. It was an important decision. This would be my new identity, the person I would be for the rest of my life. To my ears, the name Schaug sounded strange in English. And to get reconnected with my

## Chapter Fifteen

mother by sharing her last name was not a real option for me. So, I wouldn't be Schaug. And I definitely wouldn't keep Mario's last name. My other option: Fehlis.

Despite my father's repugnant past, I had good feelings about the Fehlis family I'd found in Germany. They had embraced me into their fold. I decided to become a Fehlis. I would take the name of the Gestapo father I'd never known. My Tante Eva hit the roof when I told her. She would have preferred I take her name—Hunstad. I could feel the steam coming out of her ears all the way across the Atlantic. She couldn't understand for one second why I wanted to become Fehlis. As a legal process was involved in officially changing my name, I decided to go a stage further and change my first name, too, from Wenche to Venke, mainly because a "wench" in English slang can mean a servant girl or prostitute. And although it's not common, Venke is a traditional Norwegian name. Changing my name was like changing my identity. It was a new me.

For the first few months after the divorce, though, I was completely miserable. I felt numb, mentally and physically deadened. To earn a living and keep occupied, I got a job at the front desk of a hotel. Then I went to night school and took a course to become an administrative assistant. After a year or so, I felt comfortable going out with friends and, one night, met a man who asked me for a dinner date. I hesitated because he was Jewish and I insisted that we meet for breakfast first. I felt obliged to tell him who my father was. I hadn't talked about it with anyone in a long time, but it seemed like it would be a negative factor in a potential relationship. Of course, he was a little taken aback, but he was open minded enough to appreciate that there was nothing I could do about my parentage and I had no reason to feel guilt by association. We began dating. He opened a whole new world for me and made me laugh out loud, enjoy sex, and even for the first time, when I was in my forties, say "Fuck!"

Venke with her mother, Lillemor Schaug

Venke's father, Heinrich Fehlis, and half-brother Peter, 1938-1939

Venke's mother and Venke, age 3, in Oslo, 1948

Venke, 3 years old

The Fehlis family, Wuppertal, circa 1916-1917

Venke's father, Heinrich Fehlis, in civilian clothing, 1939

Heinrich Fehlis, chief of Gestapo in Norway, 1940-1945

Venke's second stepfather, Odd Fridtjof Gustafson, Munch Museum, 1965

— 101

Venke's mother, Lillemor Schaug, Oslo, 1951

Venke and Uncle Ingolf, Aachen, Germany, 1986

Venke, on right, and Ingeborg, 1986

Peter, with his wife, Gitta, on his right, and his mother, Wally, on his left, at Hendricks's wedding, 1996

Venke in Bunad costume, age 35

Venke's passport photo, age 12

Venke's passport photo, age 20

Peter and Venke at Joe and Trudy's wedding, Westport, CT

Venke and Mario, Acapulco, Mexico, 1982

Venke and Frank, Milford, CT, 1995

# Chapter Sixteen

In 1990, two years after my divorce, I went back to Germany, and took Joe with me. We were both eager for him to get to know our family there. This time they had a big surprise in store. They'd arranged for us to meet Peter's mother, Wally Noot.

During my first visit to Aachen they had not told her anything about me, even though she lived nearby. Perhaps they felt they needed to scrutinize me first, or they were worried that meeting the daughter of her husband's mistress would be too much of a shock for her, but now they had paved the way for a get-together. How wonderful!

Wally was eighty years old and still an elegant, vivacious lady. I couldn't help but compare her favorably with Lillemor. She had remarried after the war. Her second husband was my father's closest coworker and friend, Obersturmbannführer Herbert Noot, who had been head of the German Security

Services in Norway. His department worked hand in glove with the Gestapo, but also oversaw German civilian personnel operating in the country.

During the war, Noot became increasingly critical of the hard line taken by Josef Terboven and had formed contacts with the Norwegian resistance movement. After the war, he cooperated with the Allies. According to Peter, if there was such a thing as a good Nazi, it was his stepfather, Noot. The former Obersturmbannführer was a fair and decent man, but he was always looking over his shoulder, afraid that his wartime activities would catch up with him.

Sadly, Herbert Noot had died since my previous visit to Aachen. If only I'd had the chance to sit down with him, I could have learned much more about my mother and father's wartime romance. He knew more than anyone else. He was there at my father's side. He must have socialized with Fehlis and Lillemor. He would have known what was going on. I'd gathered Fehlis's enchantment with a beautiful young Norwegian girl was not something he had gone out of his way to hide. Maybe Noot had seen me as a newborn baby and maybe even held me in his arms? My mind flashed back through everything I'd learned about the closing days of the war. What a lost opportunity to get a firsthand account.

Naturally, Wally was a little reserved when Peter introduced us. She had every right to feel strange about meeting the daughter her husband had created with another woman. And yet Wally was amazingly gracious

## Chapter Sixteen

and welcoming with no hint of resentment or hostility.

Peter had to translate because she didn't speak English or Norwegian and I only speak a little German, but she immediately exclaimed how Joe, now a handsome young man of twenty-two, looked just like Fehlis. He looked more like his grandfather than Peter and I put together, she insisted. She was completely enamored with Joe because he reminded her so much of Fehlis. Sitting at the table I politely asked if I could have another glass of wine. Wally smiled and said, "Like mother, like daughter." Wow. How did she know Lillemor liked a drink? That surprised me.

Wally was so entranced by Joe that one day on a family outing, which required two cars, she burst into tears when she learned she and Joe would not be in the same car. "He thinks I'm an old lady," she protested. It was quickly arranged that she and Joe would not be separated for the rest of our stay.

### Wonderful Wally

I couldn't help but contrast Wally—such a polite, charming older woman—with my mother who'd become an alcoholic mess. After dinner one evening, she went up to the second floor of Peter's house and came back with a letter in her hand. When she opened it, I was shocked to recognize my mother's handwriting—and a photo of me, aged about one. Lillemor had obviously felt the need, for whatever reason, to make Wally aware of her relationship with Fehlis and that a daughter had been born of it.

What exactly did the letter say? I wish I knew. Wally didn't read it to me. She didn't say if she had replied to it, and I didn't feel I had the right to pry. She was more concerned with showing me my baby photo than anything else. But I was totally perplexed. How did she discover how to contact Wally? What was there for Lillemor to gain by telling her of my existence? Could she have done it out of spite? Why send a photo of me to her lover's wife?

That was the closest we came to discussing Lillemor and Fehlis, and we certainly didn't talk about Fehlis's role in the Gestapo. It wasn't appropriate. We were all more than aware of the strange circumstances that linked us together, and there was a tacit understanding that there was no need to poke too deeply into the past. Peter also took us to meet Fehlis's sister (my aunt) and my cousins. We didn't get the same warm welcome. I got the impression they were seeing us out of curiosity more than anything else. They just wanted to check us out. The whole thing made them a little uncomfortable.

In contrast, Wally was such a classy lady and demonstrated touching acts of thoughtfulness and kindness by giving me two tangible connections to my father. One day, she presented me with a beautiful, antique ring that Fehlis had given her. It's a treasured possession that I've worn countless times. Then, the evening before we left Aachen, she made the ultimate gesture. After dinner, Joe and I gave her a lift home and she invited us into her apartment because she had something else she wanted to give me.

Wally took down a large picture from the wall, a framed drawing of my father, in full uniform, dated 1936. It was her way of acknowledging me as one of her husband's

## Chapter Sixteen

children. She wanted me to take home an object that meant something special to her. It was her way of embracing us. I couldn't help but wonder how charismatic Fehlis must have been. My mother had kept a photograph of Fehlis on her wall, even when she was married to Odd. Wally had done the same thing when she was married to Herbert Noot. It was now forty-six years since Fehlis had killed himself, but the drawing of him still had pride of place on her wall.

What kind of man was Fehlis? How did he have such a hold on Lillemor and Wally? They both knew the crimes against humanity he must have committed as a prominent member of the Nazis and chief of Gestapo in Norway, but they must have seen something else in him. I returned to the States, reflecting on this conundrum. (And today I have the drawing in its original frame hanging in my home!)

Overall, my second trip to Germany was a monumental success. I'd cemented the relationship with Peter and his family. I'd become acquainted with Wally. And I'd gleaned even more about my mother and father. There was much I still didn't know, but I'd begun to put together the story of how I came into the world at such a turbulent time.

# Chapter Seventeen

Lillemor was in a bad way.

Not long after returning to the States, I got an alarming call from Norway. Tante Eva told me that Lillemor had been drinking herself into a stupor. Tante Berit got her signed into a psychiatric hospital but somehow Lillemor had signed herself out. I hadn't even known she was in such an institution.

Lillemor had spiraled into a dark place after the death of her husband, Fred, about three months earlier. Fred had collapsed and died of a major heart attack, but Lillemor insisted no one inform me. We hadn't talked in years and I assumed it was just another way she thought she could punish me and keep me distant from the family. Lillemor had met Fred at a rehabilitation center where he had been recovering from a heart operation. She was there because she'd suffered a nervous breakdown following her divorce

## Chapter Seventeen

from Odd. Many years earlier she and Fred had attended the same secondary school. They recognized each other and reconnected. A sincere relationship quickly developed and they married not long after they were both released.

Fred was a good and kind man. Lillemor was lucky to have found him, and the fifteen or so years they were together were the best years she ever had. Fred once told me that Lillemor viewed the war years through rose-colored glasses. He was probably right. Fred tried hard to keep Lillemor's drinking under control. He would do anything to help her but, after he died, Lillemor no longer had someone to watch over her, and her drinking ratcheted out of control. It didn't take her long to hit rock bottom. Lillemor was her own worst enemy. She drank from morning to night and manipulated taxi drivers to take her to the liquor store. She said she'd bought a revolver to protect herself because all of Norway was coming to get her. Apparently, she suffered from paranoia and anxiety and was a danger to herself.

One day, Lillemor's friend, Ingjerd, whom she'd also met in rehab, found her in a pool of blood. That's when Tante Berit got her admitted into the psychiatric hospital. Ideally, Lillemor should have been checked into a Betty Ford-type clinic for alcoholics, but there was nowhere like that in Norway in those days.

Lillemor refused to stay there and, after just a week, signed herself out. That was when the family decided they had to alert me to what was going on. I immediately canceled a long-planned ski trip to Lake Tahoe and got to Norway as fast as I could. Within a couple of days, I was back in Oslo, and, as soon as I walked into Lillemor's apartment, I realized the situation was worse than I'd feared. It was the same apartment Lillemor had lived in with Fred, in a nice suburb of the city, but now it was dark, gloomy and dirty; there was an aura of sadness. Lillemor was terribly thin, just wasting away. Skin and bones. Except for her bloated stomach, which reminded me of photos I'd seen of starving children in Biafra. She'd lost a lot of hair, and the hair that remained was thin and lank. It was excruciatingly painful to see her in such bad shape.

### REUNION WITH LILLEMOR

That first night we sat at the kitchen table like two old friends, talking and catching up on the news. We drank the vodka I'd bought at the duty-free store and, although I felt a little guilty, I knew she would drink whether I was there or not. There were no recriminations, no opening of old wounds. No anger, no resentment. Just filling each other in on the lost years. How's Joe? What's he doing? Questions like that. Mostly, she reminisced about the good days she'd had with Fred whom she adored. We never talked about Fehlis. The subject was taboo because I knew she would fly into a rage if I dared to mention his name. That chapter of her life was closed for her, even if it wasn't closed for me.

She seemed happy to see me; to have me there to take care of her; to bathe her. But we couldn't stay "friends" for long. We soon locked horns. Our years of contention could not be easily papered over. As she'd gotten older, Lillemor had become

## Chapter Seventeen

meaner and nastier the more she drank. And after the bottle of vodka was empty and I refused to buy any more, the mean, nasty, insulting Lillemor soon reappeared. One morning I got up and she was standing in a corner of the room stabbing the large drinks cabinet with a kitchen knife. I wasn't scared of her attacking me, but her behavior was getting out of control. I tried to stop her drinking by threatening if she did not pull herself together, she would be sent back to the mental hospital. Even though she was terrified of going there, the threat wasn't enough to stop her drinking.

I tried to get her to pray, just like her mother had got me to pray. I would say, "Please fold your hands and pray, Lillemor," echoing how Mamma had encouraged me when I was a little girl. But Lillemor was a diehard atheist. She wouldn't pray. How could there be a God, she'd repeatedly question, when there are so many starving children in this world? For us to spend time together was not a good idea. It didn't take me a week to realize that I couldn't continue trying to look after her. I could not stay with her all the time; I had to get back to the States. The best and most willing person to help her was her sister, my Tante Eva.

Lillemor wouldn't have anything to do with her. She'd fallen out with Eva and they weren't talking. Then I came up with a plan. With Tante Eva's agreement, I made a big deal out of telling Lillemor that Eva was the one person who really didn't think Lillemor should go back to the psychiatric hospital. Hearing that, Lillemor's face lit up and, not long afterward, she suggested inviting Tante Eva and Uncle Kaare to dinner. Lillemor soon forgot why she had been angry at Eva in the first place and they reconciled. Mission accomplished, I returned to the States, and Tante Eva stepped in to take care of Lillemor.

### A Life is Over

Sadly, my mother's condition rapidly deteriorated and, within a matter of weeks, Tante Eva had to arrange for her to enter a nursing home. After a thorough examination, a doctor gave them the harsh verdict: she had about three months to live. She didn't make it that long. She died the next day, aged sixty-seven, an atheist right up until the end.

I went back to Norway for the funeral. I stood looking at her wasted body lying in a casket before she was cremated. I really didn't want to see her like that. I'd never seen a dead person before, and I was a little uptight about the experience. But I didn't feel any sadness. Lillemor was my mother in name only. I was glad her tortured life was over. She couldn't carry on the way she was living; alcohol had destroyed her. Her death, however, meant that whatever slim chance there had been of getting more information from her about my father and their doomed wartime romance was finally gone.

Lillemor hated church bells. I think that's because church bells rang all over Norway when the country got its freedom from Nazi rule while, for her, the ringing of the bells signaled her time with Fehlis was coming to an end. Later, Dr. Larson told me that she'd probably died so soon after the doctor's pronouncement because she had finally received "permission" to die.

## Chapter Seventeen

The astute Dr. Larson once said, "If it had not been for your grandmother you would not be alive today."

I believe he was right. Mamma was the one who baked cookies and gave me contraceptive advice (well, she told me that if I kissed a boy, I would have a baby). She was the one who took me to the church that was just around the corner both to attend services and social functions. In her later years, she became blind and lived in a nursing home. When she was about ninety, I got a phone call from Tante Eva, "Mamma's not doing too well. You'd better come home."

A few days later, I walked down a long, dark corridor at the nursing home and found her sitting alone on a bench, a halo of light from a window streaming around her. She had her head resting in her hand, leaning on her knee, staring into nothingness. It was the same way I had seen her sit so many, many times over the years. I knelt in front of her, placed a hand gently on her knee, and said, "Mamma, it's Venke."

She touched my head, delicately ran her fingers over my features, and asked, "Venke, is it really you?"

I still get tears in my eyes when I think about that day.

Lillemor did not inspire such tender memories and, now that she was gone, Tante Eva and I went through all of her personal effects. Buried between piles of paper we discovered a pawn ticket. Curious, we redeemed the ticket and were handed a thick gold necklace. I immediately recognized it as one Lillemor had worn day and night, a gift from Odd. I knew she had passed it on to her friend from rehab, Ingjerd, who was about my age. I'd seen her wearing it when I'd visited Norway for Tante Berit's son's graduation and had taken it as a slight against me because that was the kind of thing Lillemor did. She gave her friend something precious that most mothers would give to their daughters.

Lillemor must have gotten it back from Ingjerd so she could pawn it and get money for drink. What else? After the funeral, I invited Ingjerd for lunch and hid the necklace inside a napkin. When she opened it, she was surprised and thrilled. Tears came to her eyes, as I said, "I want you to have it, Ingjerd. It was given to you and you should keep it as a memory of Lillemor."

When we parted Ingjerd told me reassuringly, "You are not your mother's daughter, Venke. Lillemor chose to live the life she did." Left unsaid, but understood, was, "And Venke, you should live yours."

Dr. Larson once explained Lillemor's behavior toward me: "Every time your mother looked at you, she recalled the wrong she had done." Now she was gone and would look no more.

# Chapter Eighteen

I began to plan what I should do with the rest of my life. It was time for a fresh start. Could I start my own business? After all, I had twenty years' experience helping to manage a large company, handling its finances. Why couldn't I do my own thing?

My dream was to open an upmarket relaxation spa for both women and men offering a wide range of treatments and therapies. I secured a large loan from a local bank to do just that, and I investigated a cellulite reduction machine called "Thermo Trim." I first saw this machine in a beautiful Fifth Avenue salon whose owner was Swedish. She was an American success story and we hit it off right away. After ten years in business she'd saved $250,000 but, unfortunately, her husband had drained her bank account and run off with another woman, just two weeks before we met. We could relate to each other. Next, I visited the famous La Costa spa in San Diego and checked out a machine that golfers used for back problems.

On my return to Connecticut, I looked for the perfect venue and was introduced to Eva Jensch, a designer of many famous spa resorts, who became a good friend. I hired Eva to design my Greenwich day spa anti-stress center, which I called "BodiFerier"—in Norwegian and some other languages this translates as "Body Vacation." I set up rooms for facials and diverse types of massage, even installing a deep tub for underwater massage. I offered seminars on nutrition and diet and the way stress impacts the whole body.

For two years, I struggled to make the business profitable until the Fontana brothers arrived on the scene and things began to turn around. Hairdressers from the West coast, they'd worked for Jose Eber, a sought-after stylist to the stars. My friend Turi gave me a loan to turn part of the spa into a hairdressing salon and help me achieve my dream. I'll never forget when we got together to discuss the loan and she warmly clasped my hand and said, "Little friend, I want you to be successful, too."

The Fontana brothers, especially the older brother, Richard, were a big hit, and business boomed—until a year or so later they decided to move to Las Vegas and open their own salon. Although I immediately hired another high-profile hair stylist, it was never the same. Business declined and Turi stepped in again to help me out financially. A stockbroker friend worked out a deal with the landlord in which I took over larger premises in the same building at a low rent in return for improving that space. But it was not meant to be. The business fell apart, and eventually I was evicted. All that I had tried to build was gone.

Had it not been for Frank I don't know what I would have done. Frank and I had been dating for a long time. I'd met him when I was going to bars and restaurants at night with women who worked for me at the spa. We handed out flyers and brochures listing the facials, massages, and other services we provided. Frank was handsome and kind and in a troubled relationship: his wife was sleeping with the entire neighborhood while he usually stayed home looking after their two boys. After he and his wife parted company, and our romance blossomed, he asked me to move in with him, something he had always wanted. He was such a decent guy. Now I'd lost everything, I was grateful for his thoughtfulness. He was understanding and provided shelter. A port in a storm.

**SPLIT WITH FRANK**

For a few weeks, I wallowed in my misery, drinking far too much. When I came to my senses and realized I had to get back on my own two feet, I got a job selling Cadillacs at an auto dealership in Stamford, Connecticut. Frank was doing well with his printing business. As time went by, however, I realized we both had a drinking problem. I'd come home from work and he would be passed out on the couch. When I'd been wrapped up in my own misfortunes, I hadn't recognized he had an addiction to alcohol. It got so bad that an entire week could pass without him going to work. Frank burned through what money we had. I had to be the strong one. If we didn't stop drinking, we were going to lose everything we possessed.

I managed to curb my consumption, but he was unwilling to help himself. The demon drink changed Frank from a gentle, considerate man to someone who became threatening. Frank had been my rock when my life was at its lowest ebb. He picked me up from the depths of despair, but now he was at his lowest there was only so much I could do for him. He had sunk too far. He needed professional help. Joe, his wife Trudy, and their three boys, were going to move to California and I told Frank that if he didn't quit, I would go with them. Even that ultimatum didn't bring him to his senses. He couldn't stop drinking, just like my mother had not been able to quit. I had to get out. Joe and his wife came to the rescue and I lived with them for a while. Joe paid off some of Frank's debts and Frank moved into his parents' basement. After four years, our relationship was at an end, destroyed by drink.

During the time that life with Frank was rapidly disintegrating, Mario briefly reentered my life. We hadn't spoken for over eight years, so I was shocked to get a call from him. Within seconds all the bad memories flooded back. His voice full of venom, he said, "Hey, Venke, I just want you to know that here you are selling cars and I've sold the business for $12 million." It was the same old boastful, arrogant, vindictive Mario. It epitomized the nature of the man.

His real reason for calling, he said, was to suggest that he and I and Joe get together to celebrate Joe's upcoming

## Chapter Eighteen

thirtieth birthday. For Joe's sake, I agreed. But during the lunch, it soon became obvious why Mario wanted me there—it was so I could witness him present Joe with an expensive Rolex watch for his birthday. Beyond that, it turned into an occasion for Mario to berate and belittle me, just like he'd done during our marital years. He was as sarcastic as he'd ever been. I did not defend myself, because it was Joe's day and I didn't want to make a scene in the restaurant.

The encounter was too much for Joe who suddenly began to cry. It was terribly painful to see my grown son reduced to tears at his thirtieth birthday celebration in the middle of a fine restaurant. It dawned on me how much our divorce had hurt him, something I had not truly considered before, gripped so much in my own pain. But it was more than that. Mario had been a parasite in Joe's soul, tormenting him during the five years Joe had worked for him, psychologically manipulating him while blaming me for the marital breakup. And Mario hadn't given him a penny of the $12 million he'd got for selling the business but lavished it all on his new family. Joe had been under too much pressure to protect me from his self-absorbed, narcissistic dad and it all came crashing to a head. Mario was unresponsive. He barely moved a muscle and sat there emotionless. I couldn't get out of the restaurant fast enough, determined never to have anything to do with this man again. Where was the independent strong-minded woman I thought I'd become? Luckily, an event soon followed that boosted my self-confidence.

## Chapter Nineteen

The wedding invitation was more than a wedding invitation. If ever I needed confirmation that I was a welcomed member of my father's German family, this was it. Peter's son, Hendricks, was getting married in Aachen, and the family wanted me to attend. I felt wonderfully embraced. It was a bright spot in my life coming after the break-up of my four-year relationship with Frank and the business failure that ended in bankruptcy. It took a nanosecond for me to decide to make the journey.

Joe couldn't go with me because of business commitments, so I traveled alone. Hendricks was so obviously delighted at my presence, it gave me a delicious, joyous feeling of being included. It had been almost ten years since my previous visit and I was thrilled to be able to reconnect not only with Peter and Hendricks, but also Uncle Ingolf and Ingeborg.

## Chapter Nineteen

After my stay in Aachen, I went on to visit Tante Eva and Uncle Kaare in Oslo for a few days. I told Tante Eva I was thinking of writing a book about my mother and father and the events of May 1945—the "horse trade" saga as it was dubbed in the newspaper.

"Really?" said Tante Eva. "I had no idea you were that interested. If you want to know more about your mother, you should read this."

She handed me a book titled *Cupido Og Det Gamle Apotek* (*Cupid and the Old Pharmacy*), the memoir of Gerd Høst Heyerdahl—"Tante Gerd," my mother's friend, the actress whose photos I'd admired as a child, the woman I'd listened to on the radio, entranced as she taught German.

I opened the hardcover book and there, to my surprise, was an entire chapter simply titled "Lillemor." It provided a plethora of detail about a time in my mother's life that no one else knew and that I'd never heard before.

It told the story of how Gerd had first met Lillemor in Oslo during the last year of the war and again, accidentally, in Stockholm, a few weeks after the war had ended. Their first encounter was at the Gestapo headquarters at Oslo's Victoria Terrasse, an address that became synonymous with terror and oppression. Gerd, who was Norwegian, had worked in Berlin for the German movie and theater industry and spoke German fluently. She'd moved back to Norway at the outbreak of World War II and secretly worked for the Resistance. Her acting and language skills, not to mention her beauty and feminine wiles, made her the ideal person to intercede with the much-hated chief of Gestapo, Henrich Fehlis, petitioning for the release of fellow freedom fighters.

Totally fearless, Gerd waltzed past security guards and went straight to Fehlis's office. In her autobiography, she described her first meeting with my father: "If I did not know that he was the chief of the Gestapo, and responsible for the suffering and death of so many of our fellow Norwegians, I would have thought of him as a sympathetic man. He was an example of split personality between courteous behavior and the brutal terror displayed by the SS, a kind of Dr. Jekyll and Mr. Hyde."

Gerd pretended she was pleading on behalf of her boyfriend. She told Fehlis that her man was innocent and she missed him, "Bitte, bitte, please let him go free." The prisoner was released. Because of her success, the Resistance asked her to go back and ask for the release of her "boyfriend" on a few more occasions. Fehlis questioned her expansive love life, but enjoyed her boldness, and acquiesced. Once he laughed, and asked, "How many boyfriends do you have, Fraülein Høst?"

On one visit to the office, when Fehlis was absent, Gerd met a young woman alone in the front office, whom she described as "strangely beautiful." She was sitting on the edge of the desk, casually dangling a shoe that was in danger of falling off her foot. Gerd explained her mission to the woman, who said she would help. Gerd asked her name. "Call me Lillemor," was the response. A few days later Lillemor phoned with the news that the prisoner in question would be freed. She'd made it happen.

CHAPTER NINETEEN

Not long afterward, Gerd and her family fled Norway for the safety of Sweden. Their anti-German activities were on the verge of being revealed and it was getting too dangerous for them in Oslo. Gerd began working in Stockholm for the Legion Office of Escapees, work which continued throughout the summer of 1945.

One beautiful sunny day as she walked along Kungsgatan (King's Street), a main thoroughfare, "in a sleepy, happy mood," Gerd heard her name being called. She turned around and saw a young woman pushing a baby stroller. There was something familiar about the face, but she couldn't quite place it.

"It's Lillemor," the woman said.

"Lillemor?" asked Gerd.

"Don't you remember me? At Fehlis's office. I managed to get the prisoner freed. Have you really forgotten that?"

Gerd had not forgotten. Lillemor was "just as beautiful" as she remembered, but looked tired, and "her eyes were red and lifeless as if she had cried all night or not been able to sleep." Lillemor told Gerd that the sleeping baby in the stroller was hers. She desperately needed to talk.

"I need to speak with you, but not here. Let's find a place where we can sit uninterrupted," she said looking around nervously and, with a sense of urgency, almost dragged Gerd to the nearest park.

They found a bench and sat down. Lillemor immediately pulled out a pack of cigarettes and, with shaking hands, lit one. She had been through a heart-wrenching ordeal and needed to unburden herself and in Gerd she'd found a willing, sympathetic audience, a good listener. Lillemor confessed her relationship with Fehlis and that the Gestapo chief was the father of her child. She spoke for hours, nervously puffing on one cigarette after another, alternately coughing and crying. When baby Venke finally awoke and started crying, Lillemor stood up and Gerd followed as she hurriedly pushed the stroller back to the boarding house where we lived. It was late on a Friday afternoon. Lillemor and Gerd met again the next day and the day after and Lillemor continued to pour out her story.

## GET-TOGETHER WITH GERD

Here was information I'd never heard before, laid out in a book, no less, written by someone who'd had an intimate connection with my mother. I needed to know more. I had to meet the author, Tante Gerd. But how could I find her? Where was she? And would she be willing to talk to me? As it happened, it couldn't be any simpler; she was listed in the telephone directory. I wasted no time calling her, explained who I was, and that I was returning to the States in two days. Could we meet? Gerd invited me to her home for tea the next day.

She greeted me at the door of her apartment, situated in a nice section of Oslo. A slim, elegant, older woman. The first words out of her mouth: "Did you know I'm the one who saved your life?" I knew, of course, from the newspaper article I'd been shown in Aachen years before that Lillemor had tried to kill herself. But it had not mentioned that my life had also been in danger. Now, I was about to get a shocking eye-witness account.

## Chapter Twenty

Gerd, the perfect hostess, asked if I'd prefer a cup of tea or a glass of champagne. Champagne, she said, was my mother's preference. I settled for tea, and we sat down on the sofa surrounded by solid, older furniture of exceptional quality.

Gerd knew of my mother's upbringing on the wrong side of the tracks in 1930s Norway. Lillemor, she said, dreamed of a better life, the kind portrayed in the glossy magazines she loved to read featuring glamorous women and sophisticated men, opulent villas and luxury cars. She studied the pictures and tried to fix her clothes to emulate those worn by the beautiful women. Lillemor's family was poor—and they would be poor whether there was peace or war.

After the Nazi invasion, she met Fehlis and moved in with him, a diabolical act of treachery as far as most

Norwegians were concerned. She hid the relationship from her family who lived in the same city, consorting with one of the occupiers and living a good life, much better for sure than most of her countrymen.

Lillemor knew Fehlis was married and had a son back in Germany. She didn't care. She knew he was chief of Gestapo, and she didn't care. She was so captivated by him and so deeply in love with him that nothing else mattered to her. Fehlis proudly showed her off at private dinners for German officers but she wasn't allowed to be on his arm at public events. As long as she got to stay with him, she didn't care.

Gerd added, "All she cared about was that he was her man, and she was his woman. He was her one and only. Whatever they tried to say about him, she didn't believe."

They had a loving relationship. Only once did he get angry with her, really angry, and that was when she spied on a clandestine meeting he held at their home. Lillemor sensed in advance that this meeting was going to be important, and her curiosity got the better of her. She used a set of extra keys to sneak by the guards, tiptoed to the door of the meeting room, and peeked through a keyhole. To her surprise, she saw the chief justice of the supreme court, Paal Berg, and other Norwegians she did not recognize. (Berg was reputedly the secret leader of the Resistance. Whether Fehlis knew this or not is open to question.) Perhaps luckily for her she could not hear the conversation.

A few days later, Lillemor confessed to Fehlis what she had done. His face turned pale with fright and then red with anger. After his anger died down, he explained that

## Chapter Twenty

in war one needed to have contact with the enemy and she had to promise to never, ever reveal what she had seen. But the war was over and Fehlis was dead and she had to unburden herself, said Gerd.

They were both happy when she became pregnant with me. Their time waiting for my birth went by like a dream. When I was born, Fehlis, in a rare display of emotion, held me in his arms and cried. The tide of war had turned against Germany and he worried what the future had in store for them. If they were captured, the likely penalty was death for him and imprisonment for her. Day after day, night after night, they agonized over their options.

"They both knew that their days together were numbered and spent as much time together as they could," said Gerd.

Fehlis made it clear that if he could not escape, he would have to commit suicide. He could not be taken alive. Lillemor argued for a suicide pact. They would go together.

Gerd recalled, "She wanted to die with him and to bring the little child to her mother who would take good care of her. But he said no; she was too young to die. For her, the future had possibility, but not for him."

Fehlis came up with a plan, which I had already read about in newspaper accounts. I knew about the secret negotiations with the Swedish criminalist, Harry Söderman, who was concerned about the fate of thousands of Norwegian prisoners held by the Germans. When peace came, Söderman wanted Fehlis to arrange for the gates at Grini Detention Camp and Mollergaten 19 to be opened and the prisoners set free without any retaliation.

## Venke

Lillemor fought against the plan to arrange safe passage for her and the baby, but Fehlis persuaded her it was the only way, explained Gerd. If we were smuggled out, he could go underground and try to escape. Who knew what could happen? Maybe he would be able to join us in Sweden in a year or two. It was spring; it would soon be summer. The weather turned fine and the sunshine gave Lillemor hope for the future. Exhausted and exasperated, she finally acquiesced, and events moved quickly. Fehlis reached an agreement with Söderman, who arranged for our transportation in a chauffeur-driven government car.

At an appointed time, Lillemor walked down the steps from their home and into a large, black limo idling at the curb. Fehlis followed behind carrying me close to his chest before bending down and carefully handing me into her waiting arms. I already knew his parting words: "If the worst happens, please know that in my last minutes I will think of you and only you. Remember that. Only you."

Tante Gerd heard the details of this emotional parting firsthand from Lillemor's own lips.

Söderman took us to Stockholm and found a room for us at a boarding house. For the first few weeks, Lillemor told Gerd, she walked around in a daze without any feeling of time and place. She was so traumatized, she stopped producing breast milk. Then the worst news of all: she heard a dramatic radio announcement of the death by suicide of the notorious Gestapo chief, Heinrich Fehlis.

CHAPTER TWENTY

**FEHLIS'S FUTILE BID TO ESCAPE**

What exactly happened to Fehlis? I found out from other sources that, back in Norway, after the limo bearing Lillemor and me had headed for Sweden, Fehlis drove to the Gestapo headquarters at Furulund, on the west side of Oslo. The scene was chaotic: a mad scramble to flee the wrath of the Norwegian Resistance. The seventy-five men who remained there, out of an original force of seven hundred, knew they would quickly become the most hunted men in the country. Revenge for their brutal suppression of the local population would be exacted. They would probably not escape with their lives. On the morning of May 10, Fehlis and those seventy-five men drove in a convoy of twenty-five automobiles from Oslo to Heistadmoen, close to Kongsberg.

At Heistadmoen, they ditched their Gestapo uniforms and changed into uniforms of the Swiss Alpine Division of the Wehrmacht and were issued with paperwork supporting their false identities. From there they traveled on by train to the southern harbor town of Porsgrunn and moved into the Lager Franken military camp. Unfortunately for Fehlis, a young German, who was ordered to burn the Gestapo uniforms behind the barracks, took the opportunity to escape. Captured in the local chief of police's backyard, he revealed what had happened.

The Gestapo were regarded as war criminals and the surrender agreement forbade anyone—including regular German soldiers—to hide or shelter them. The Norwegian authorities, with the cooperation of the defeated German military leadership, was determined not to let Fehlis and his Gestapo men slip through the net. They swiftly surrounded the camp and demanded to meet with him. Fehlis presented himself as Lieutenant Gerstheuer of the Swiss Alpine Division, but they weren't fooled so easily and put him on the phone to a superior officer, who promptly ordered him to surrender. Fehlis's request for an hour to organize his men was granted.

One hour later, when the Norwegians entered the camp, they encountered a group of drunken Gestapos who had obviously hit the bottle hard, but Fehlis was not among them. They searched the barracks and found him in a locked room, dead, his body sprawled on a bed. He had taken poison and shot himself in the head, and his pistol lay beside him.

Lillemor became despondent because she had not died with her lover.

"It was wrong of me," she told Gerd. "We should have died together and then the little one would have a better life without me."

Gerd tried to console Lillemor and spoke about the endless possibilities of life and never giving up, until she realized how shallow it sounded.

"What possibilities?" Lillemor asked Gerd, one day in the park. "What can I expect from life? My relationship with Fehlis will always put a mark on me. I cannot hide forever. There will come a time when I will be forced to reveal myself. And then what? What about the little one?"

The little one was sitting in the stroller keeping an eye on the birds and screaming with delight.

CHAPTER TWENTY

Lillemor insisted she wanted to die. That was the best solution.

She told Gerd, "The little one will have a good life with my mother. She never needs to find out who her father was."

Gerd persuaded her to do nothing until she could speak with Lillemor's mother, something that was not so easy in those days. Communication between Sweden and Norway in 1945 was not a simple matter of picking up a phone.

Lillemor had not seen much of Harry Söderman since he'd smuggled her out of Norway, but his mother and sister were concerned about her wellbeing and visited her at the boarding house. She had some money —but it was running out. When Gerd's roommate and friend, a fellow member of the Resistance, moved back to Norway, Lillemor asked if she could share her apartment. The boarding house was expensive and she was lonely. She could get a job and find a babysitter for Venke, she said, but before she could do anything, she had to get Harry Söderman's permission.

Gerd greatly anticipated meeting the famous "Revolver Harry," an owlish, bespectacled chain-smoking cop with a reputation as an intellectual. "Proper" and "correct" were other words used to describe him. Gerd found Söderman to be friendly, even charming, but also inscrutable. It was hard to tell what he was thinking as he sized her up and his eyes roamed around the apartment. Söderman knew she was aware of Lillemor's entire story and they spoke openly about it. Then he gave his approval for Lillemor and me to move in.

Venke

At first everything went well. Lillemor seemed at peace with herself. She took me for long walks. She began to care about her appearance, and had her hair and nails done. She cooked delicious dinners that awaited Gerd's return in the evenings. Sometimes, she was even able to laugh. Then, one night, things took a dramatic turn for the worse.

According to Gerd: "I was woken abruptly out of my sleep. My head was hurting; the apartment was filled with a sickeningly sweet smell. I raced to the kitchen." Lillemor had her head and the baby's head (my head!) inside the gas oven.

"I dragged her away," said Gerd. "I turned off the gas, opened all the windows to let fresh air in, and pulled mother and baby toward the window. You were blue in the face but you soon opened your eyes and smiled."

Lillemor, pale and drained, looked at Gerd and, in a small, tired voice, asked, "Why did you stop me?"

## Chapter Twenty-One

"Yes, I saved your life," said Gerd. I finally learned, while drinking tea out of a china cup with an elegant eighty-year-old woman in a beautifully furnished Oslo apartment, that my mother had not only tried to kill herself but me as well. Gerd disclosed one stunning revelation after another. It brought home to me the absolute wretchedness my mother had suffered.

Over the years Lillemor had doled out tidbits of the story. Truths, half-truths, misrepresentations, and outright lies. I'd certainly gleaned trustworthy information from my German family, and the newspaper articles published in Norway and Sweden had been enlightening. But what I'd learned from those sources paled in comparison with the vivid firsthand account Gerd was able to provide.

My mother and I had moved in with her not long after Fehlis's suicide. Lillemor trusted Gerd and confided in her.

She was the one friend who could understand Lillemor's anguish. Gerd knew me when I was a little baby. She knew me before Tante Eva and Tante Berit, before Mamma and Pappa, and any of my relatives had a chance to meet me. Being with Gerd was a surreal experience.

Gerd poured another cup of tea, and continued with her story. Lillemor was not happy that Gerd had stopped her from gassing us to death. Shortly after the horrific attempt, however, she fell into a listless sleep. For Gerd, there was no sleep. She was afraid what Lillemor might do next. She drank cup after cup of coffee to stay awake and keep a clear head. In a few hours, she would have to go to work and she did not dare leave Lillemor and me alone. There was only one thing she could do. At daylight, she called Söderman and described the grim events of the night before.

Immediately, "Revolver Harry" came over and took us away with him, telling Gerd he'd let her know what became of us. But he didn't. Worried sick, Gerd managed to get hold of him three days later, and he reported that Lillemor had been admitted to Beckomberga; baby Venke was being cared for by his mother and sister.

Beckomberga? Wasn't that an insane asylum? Yes, but Söderman insisted Lillemor was in a quiet, secluded part of the hospital where she could rest and recuperate. She was all right. She was in good hands. Gerd wasn't convinced. As soon as she got off the phone, she called the hospital to check for herself. They wouldn't let her speak to Lillemor. They said she was ill and couldn't be brought

## Chapter Twenty-One

to the phone. But Gerd could visit? No, she was informed, visitors weren't allowed. Gerd wrote a letter to Lillemor, but didn't get a reply.

Meanwhile, Tante Eva picked me up from the Södermans and took me back to Oslo to stay with various members of my mother's family. I was looked after by my grandmother and Tante Eva, and my grandmother's sister, Signe, together with her husband, Guttorm. My grandmother was stunned. She hadn't known of my existence and that my father was chief of Gestapo—one of the worst human beings imaginable for her. But, pragmatic as ever, she accepted the reality of the situation. My grandfather's sister, Tante Kristin, with whom I also lived a couple of times, wanted to adopt me. Years later when Lillemor told me about that, I said to myself, "If only she had allowed Tante Kristin to adopt me, what a different life I would have had." At the same time, I imagined Lillemor saying, "Look what I have suffered because of you."

Some weeks after Lillemor was taken into Beckomberga, Gerd got a phone call from a nurse asking if she could visit and bring a comb. Gerd was delighted at the opportunity to see Lillemor and embarked on the rather long journey. She sat in the forbidding reception area, and, after a long wait, a barely recognizable Lillemor appeared. She walked lethargically. Her face was drawn and haggard; eyes blank; hair tangled and unwashed. They sat down in a corner away from everyone else so their conversation could not be heard.

Lillemor pleaded, "Get me out of here right now. I can't take it anymore."

# Venke

She was not in a quiet part of the hospital at all. The nights were full of frightening shouts and screams, as inmates fought their personal demons.

"They won't even let me have a comb," complained Lillemor, running her hand distractedly through her matted hair, and gratefully accepting the comb Gerd had brought with her.

Gerd was shocked, and said she would do what she could to help. True to her word, as soon as she got home, she contacted Söderman and begged him to get Lillemor released. Lillemor wasn't crazy, just someone who'd been through a terrible ordeal. She had regained her will to live. She needed love and kindness, not to be locked up in a mental asylum. Lillemor was allowed out of Beckomberga, moved in with Söderman's mother and sister, and got a job in the post office, which worked out well.

Gerd felt, though, that Lillemor would have a better future back in Norway with her own family, and, on a trip to Norway, Gerd met with Brynjulf Bull, state attorney for the government in Oslo, whom she had known from her days in the Resistance, and explained Lillemor's plight to him. Bull suggested the best course of action was for Lillemor to return to Oslo and put the episode behind her. When Lillemor followed the advice and turned herself in, she was arrested and held in prison. The authorities endlessly quizzed Lillemor about her unusual escape from Norway to Sweden. That's all they seemed interested in. "You can go home as soon as you tell us who helped you cross the border," her interrogators insisted again and

CHAPTER TWENTY-ONE

again. Lillemor steadfastly refused to give up Söderman's name and, after three weeks, they simply let her go.

**EARLY YEARS**

During these early years, I lived part of the time with my relatives in Norway. One of my first memories—I could not have been more than two years old—is standing on the window sill at Tante Signe's house, eating a soft-boiled egg and seeing horses for the first time. I had fun with Tante Signe and Uncle Guttorm. Every day when Guttorm came home from work, I ran and hid in the kitchen. "Hiding" meant that I wedged my head between the stove and the cabinet, while the rest of me was visibly sticking out. Guttorm played the game, walking around the kitchen, calling out, "Where is Venke? I can't find her!" One day, though, he had me in tears when he looked at a photo of monkeys in the Sunday newspaper and teased, "Oh, look at the monkeys. They look just like Venke." I didn't appreciate that sort of humor—it made me cry.

Gerd told me that about a year or two later, when she revisited Stockholm, she found that Lillemor had married the Russian duke, whose lineage, she believed, dated back several centuries to the time of the tsars. The duke worshipped Lillemor and me, but his love was not reciprocated. Lillemor confessed to Gerd she had married to give me a father and a home so we didn't have to continue to live under the Södermans' roof.

"Something hard had come over her," reported Gerd, who confirmed what I already knew, that the marriage didn't last long.

Venke

Maybe Lillemor married because she needed to show the Södermans she could take care of herself. Maybe she thought the duke had money. But he was penniless, too. The only items of any value he possessed were two Russian icons he'd smuggled out of the country. Lillemor later gave them to me and I still have them although, according to Christie's, where I had them valued, they're genuine but not worth very much.

Gerd and Lillemor exchanged friendly letters for a few years but contact became less frequent. The last time Gerd saw her in person was during the time she was married to Odd. She thought Lillemor seemed happier. Then Gerd moved to Trondheim, Norway's third largest city, and they lost touch. When she later returned to Oslo, she searched for Lillemor but couldn't find her. She had disappeared. She wasn't at the same address or the same place of work and Gerd didn't know Odd's last name.

Subsequently, she came across Harry Söderman's autobiography in which he detailed his part in getting the prisoners freed but strangely never mentioned the "horse trade" or Lillemor. Gerd said Söderman was the big hero, and he could tell the story any way he wanted and presumably decided that revealing the "horse trade" would have cast him in a bad light, although she did not feel it would have diminished his role or made it less meaningful. His daughter Karin kept in touch with Gerd for years. In one letter, Karin wrote, "Whatever you say about [Lillemor], she was hopelessly in love with Fehlis."

Gerd remembered Lillemor telling her, "I will try to

## Chapter Twenty-One

raise my daughter to be strong and confident so that the knowledge about her father will not break her—if she ever finds out who he was."

As we sat on the sofa drinking tea, Gerd opened another intriguing line of inquiry. She mentioned an incident she'd heard about that happened at the Norwegian Home Front Museum in Oslo, around 1980. During an exhibition, a young blond woman pointed at a photo of Fehlis that was hanging on the wall, and exclaimed, "That's my father!"

Gerd asked me, "Was that you?"

It wasn't. But it triggered the memory of the conversation years earlier in which Lillemor disclosed that I not only had a half-brother living in Germany but also alluded to a half-sister, before she abruptly ended the conversation. I'd found Peter in Aachen. Perhaps there was a sister to be found somewhere, as well? Wouldn't that be something?

Before I left Gerd, she showed me around her neat apartment. She told me there was no man in her life as a relationship "was just too much work." But she loved her computer. Every night before she went to bed, she said she gently patted it, and said goodnight. That was her relationship. She was a prolific writer, a famous personality. I was encouraged when she said it was a wonderful idea for me to write a book and offered to help as much as she could. We parted, promising to write to each other.

## Chapter Twenty-Two

Gerd had opened a Pandora's Box. The more I uncovered, the more I questioned everything I'd been led to believe. Who was telling the truth? Lillemor, it seemed, had lived in her own world. She'd created her own reality. How much she believed her own stories was open to question. Her relationship with Fehlis felt like a stain on the whole family, so it wasn't surprising that no one had volunteered information over the years. It was something that just wasn't spoken about—until I started asking uncomfortable questions.

Back at Tante Eva's I prodded her to open up, and reveal what she knew. More pieces of the puzzle fell into place. Eva had also kept secrets, even from their mother. She told me that after Lillemor finished high school at the age of eighteen, she got a job at the Gestapo headquarters in Victoria Terrasse. Despite the Germans seizing control

## Chapter Twenty-Two

of her country, she was more enamored with the men in their sharp military uniforms than the young boys with whom she'd hung out.

Lillemor was bowled over by the attentions of the tall, charming, Gestapo chief, even though, at thirty-six, he was twice her age. Before long, unknown to her family, she was living with him, until Tante Eva, discovered the truth and, unafraid of anyone, confronted Fehlis and asked him to leave Lillemor alone.

She couldn't get Fehlis to change his mind, and he made a distinct impression on her. As she made her way home, after her unsuccessful meeting, she thought to herself, "What a handsome man. No wonder Lillemor is in love with him." Tante Eva kept Lillemor's secret relationship to herself, even when she subsequently discovered that Lillemor was carrying a baby. One of her girlfriends spotted Lillemor, obviously seven to eight months pregnant, enjoying a meal in a well-known, high-class restaurant. Tante Eva resolved to definitely keep her lips sealed. This was not something to share with their parents.

After everything I'd heard about the teenage Lillemor, I pictured the famous Hollywood actress, Hedy Lamarr, in the classic Cecil B. DeMille movie, *Samson and Delilah*, especially the scene where she reclines on a chaise longue while men serve her with wine and grapes. Lillemor was beautiful and turned heads, but she was also smart—perhaps street-smart is a better way to put it. She was headstrong and manipulative. She had a sharp tongue and, in an argument, could hold her own with anyone. It seemed she was even able to wrap the chief of Gestapo around her little finger. She knew what she wanted, and she got it.

I flew back to the States armed with this new information, now seriously considering writing a book about my quest to understand more about my mother and father and the circumstances of my early years. Gerd had been encouraging, and it was a theme she repeated in her first letter to me. She wrote: "Your idea of writing a book about your father is brilliant. Go ahead! It will help you to delve into his destiny and try to find out why it went the way it did. It can be an interesting book. Be happy, little friend, and look forward to getting started."

"Little friend"—there again someone had used that Norwegian term of endearment, something I very much appreciated—and to get such words of encouragement from someone so accomplished, reiterating what she'd told me in person, was truly inspirational. I was convinced I had to research and write a book. Dr. Larson had once said to me that I would never feel good about myself until I found out something good about Fehlis. Was there anything good to discover about a man who'd been branded in *Expressen* as the "Desk Executioner"?

My half-brother, Peter, and I had talked about Fehlis, but he was only one year old when his father went to war, so he had no memory of him. Uncle Ingolf, apparently, had not spoken much about his brother. It was a touchy subject. The first time we met in Aachen, Uncle Ingolf had told me he'd only seen his brother once during the war

## Chapter Twenty-Two

years when Fehlis had made a visit to Berlin seeking to leave his position in the Gestapo.

Fehlis had asked him, "What will happen if Germany loses the war?"

Uncle Ingolf had replied, "We will all go to Hell."

It was the last time the two brothers met.

Fehlis made a second trip to Berlin, accompanied by Lillemor, but, as Ingolf was very friendly with Wally, it was not deemed appropriate to meet. Lillemor had once told me about the same trip and said that when Fehlis's superior officer, the commandant, met her, he told Fehlis, "Now I understand why you want to leave your post." Did that actually happen? The story came from Lillemor, and was obviously self-serving, so I don't know.

### The "Good" Fehlis

I wanted to know more about the person who existed before Hitler and his Nazis rose to power and the war changed everything. I wrote to Uncle Ingolf and asked if he could tell me about my father. If anyone would know, it would be he. It wasn't long before I received a lengthy, cordial response.

He wrote, "I really want to give you what you are searching for and hope you will be satisfied with what I have to tell you."

Fehlis's father, also called Heinrich, was a businessman; his mother, Anna, a farmer's daughter. She was a student cook for one of the most famous hotels in Hanover, which gave her the experience to later run the Radhuskjeller Restaurant in Wuppertal. Heinrich and Anna both died young. He was forty-eight; she was fifty-three. It was then that my father Heinrich (whom the family called Heinz) took over the responsibility of caring for his younger siblings.

Uncle Ingolf described him as an excellent student who passed all his law exams with flying colors. At university, though, he became involved with the Nazi Student organization, which brought him to the attention of the Nazi hierarchy in Berlin and led to his position in the secret police.

"Unfortunately!" bemoaned Ingolf, "Otherwise, your father would have been a lawyer, or gone into industry. What a destiny!"

Ingolf became effusive in his praise: "Our parents were proud of Heinz and his siblings worshipped him. He was the family's 'star,' [he] played the piano well, was a quiet and deliberate conversationalist, [was] well-read and with many interests. He looked impressive, 186cm. (6ft. 1in.) tall, slim and always well and appropriately dressed. His kindness to his siblings was outstanding; he was like a father to us. When our mother died in January 1933, it was he who divided the inheritance, without claiming a cent for himself. What a wonderful man!"

Ingolf went on to write, "Peter is a fine young man today. Heinz would have been proud of him."

The letter made a deep impression on me. In it, Ingolf also told me that my father's youngest brother, the youngest of four siblings, had only been five years old when their

## Chapter Twenty-Two

father died and eleven when their mother died. He was seventeen when World War II broke out. Conscripted into the army, he was killed in Russia in 1942 at Kalach-on-Don, near Stalingrad. Another tragedy in a war of tragedies.

Why had my father joined the Nazi party and the SS? I doubted I would ever get a satisfactory answer to that question. Like many Germans, he became a member of the party the same year Hitler, with his fiery rhetoric, aroused the country's nationalistic fervor and won the election. Fehlis must have seen the Nazis as a solution to the country's economic ills, something he had experienced firsthand. Fehlis had taken responsibility for his siblings and provided for their education and all their needs in the 1930s when unemployment was rife and Germany was struggling as a nation.

Ingolf's letter convinced me that I had to write a book. Uncovering the Lillemor and Fehlis story would help me unravel the vicissitudes of my own life. I continued to correspond with Gerd, and sent her a few draft pages to get her opinion, but she changed her mind and began to question whether writing a book was the right thing to do. What good would it serve? Would it stir up too many painful memories for a lot of people?

"Do you really want to put your finger in someone's wounds?" she asked.

I wondered if Gerd was concerned that I would portray her role differently to her representation of what had happened, that maybe she would seem sympathetic to

Germany and that was why she'd had second thoughts. Gerd went on to say that maybe my father had some good qualities, maybe there was a purpose in discussing the good along with the awful. How would I describe this complexity?

In one letter to Gerd, I referred to Fehlis as "the General." Gerd was quick to respond that he had never been a general; he had never been an officer in the regular army and the Gestapo did not have generals. They did not have military ranks of that kind. Perhaps not, but my birth certificate clearly stated that my father was, "General Heinrich Fehlis."

It was not, however, my original birth certificate, which had been lost, perhaps deliberately burned, along with other papers, before Lillemor and I were smuggled out of Norway. This second certificate was issued when I was four years old and after we moved back from Sweden. Gerd was disturbed that Lillemor had lied to me, even to the extent of misrepresenting my father's military rank on the birth certificate.

I was even more disturbed. For my entire life, I'd thought of my father, even after I knew he held a high-ranking position in the Gestapo, as "The General." It was a prestigious title and I thought spoke well of him. I had to wait all these years to discover my mother had misled me so much. The fact that he wasn't a general really bothered me. It gnawed away at me and made me question my own identity. In some ways, I felt diminished.

The question of my mother's marriage also arose. Lillemor had always referred to my father as her husband.

## Chapter Twenty-Two

Peter had doubted there could have been a marriage as Fehlis was still legally married to his mother. Gerd maintained there had not been an official marriage but some kind of private wedding ceremony that Fehlis had arranged to keep Lillemor happy. More discoveries. More lies. If they weren't married that made me illegitimate.

"Lillemor was a sweet and nice girl, but she lived in her own made-up world," wrote Gerd.

## Chapter Twenty-Three

Joe moved his family to Santa Barbara in November, 2002, and I made the move with them. Almost all my close Norwegian friends had left Connecticut; some to Florida, one couple to Africa, one to Seattle, and others back to Norway. The sunshine of Santa Barbara—the "American Riviera"—sounded good to me. A place to begin a new life.

Many famous people have chosen to make this idyllic city their home, including the likes of Oprah Winfrey, so why couldn't I? Unlike Oprah, however, I had to get a job—which didn't turn out to be a problem. I quickly found a dealership that was happy to hire me selling cars. Once we settled, I made up my mind to embrace the California lifestyle and learn how to meditate. It didn't take me long to find a Buddhist monk who taught meditation. At his classes, I met a very sweet young girl who suggested I

## Chapter Twenty-Three

would enjoy a weekend retreat, something I'd never considered. My initial reaction was to gracefully decline, but, as I opened my mouth to say, "No, thank you," I heard myself say, "Yes, why not?"

So, there I was, in a huge park just outside Santa Barbara, four of us sharing a sparsely furnished cabin and sleeping in bunk beds. Not the height of luxury. But I wasn't there to pamper my body. This wasn't an outing to a luxury hotel spa. I was there to nourish my mind and my soul. The hours of meditation transported me into another place, although, at one stage, I did wonder what my deeply religious Christian Mamma would say if she could see me at a Buddhist retreat. Mamma had enjoyed teasing Lillemor, an avowed atheist, by making the sign of the cross in front of her. And now I was consorting with Buddhists. Whatever next?

This retreat was special. It helped me take another step toward accepting and understanding myself. In one session, the monk explained that if you had a great fear of something—spiders, for example—you should have someone put a spider in a glass bowl on the other side of the room. Then, day by day, move the bowl closer and closer. Eventually, he maintained, you would overcome the fear. It was an apt analogy.

What was my greatest fear? Nazism. There was a lot I didn't know. I'd shunned books and movies that highlighted the atrocities the Gestapo had committed. Maybe it was time for me to be brave and explore deeper? So, I took the plunge. The first thing I did was watch Steven Spielberg's

Oscar-winning epic, *Schindler's List*. Then I bought some books. They were heavy going, revealing in gory detail the unthinkable horrors of the Holocaust. I struggled to get through them, appalled by the indecency of what humans can do to other humans. How could I summon up the fortitude to write my own book—something I had started to consider?

While living in Santa Barbara, we celebrated Norway's Independence Day, May 17, with the local Norwegian community. I couldn't help but wonder what reaction I would get from these good folks if I stood up and revealed to them the identity of my father. Would I be reviled? Would I be ostracized? Around the same time, I signed up for a writing class, but my confidence was zero. I trembled and stuttered when I told the teacher the subject I wanted to write about. Worse still, I almost choked when I had to read aloud to the rest of the class my first feeble efforts at writing. Ringing in my ears was my mother's scornful laughter and disparaging words when I was a little girl so proud of my homework.

Unfortunately, we didn't stay long in Santa Barbara but, when Joe got a wonderful promotion, moved to Pleasanton, California. I switched from selling cars to working as finance manager for the Olympic Boat Center and was soon able to move into an apartment of my own. During this time, the wine bottle became my friend again. I drank too much, for sure, yet was always able to pick myself up. But, as each year went by, I seemed to become more dependent than I had the year before.

## Chapter Twenty-Three

**Coast-to-Coast**

In 2009, after six years in Pleasanton, we did another coast-to-coast relocation and traveled back to Connecticut. What had been a comfort, became a liability. I hit sixty-five, and I was in bad mental and physical shape. I was at a crossroads and had to break this habit, so I stayed away from people and places where alcohol was served and found new friends who were non-drinkers. Little by little, I was able to do without that glass of wine. And, lo and behold, my mood became brighter; I was happier with myself.

Sad to say, I relapsed a few times. There were occasions when I felt lonely and scared and reached for a glass of wine (or two.) After all, I had been living with alcohol by my side for more than forty years. I could have a glass or two, couldn't I? It turns out I couldn't. I couldn't stop after a glass or two and the same old pattern repeated itself. Alcohol began to control me. For as long as I could remember, I'd seen my mother grab a glass of liquor when something became difficult for her. I'd watched her deteriorate over the years. The more she drank, the meaner she got. She was an angry drunk. She drank to numb her suffering; to try and assuage the sense of guilt that hovered over her. I certainly didn't want to become like her.

Luckily, my new friends came to my aid. They showed me that they cared about me. I also looked to a higher authority—Almighty God. I gave myself over to God and began to pray. When I was little, Mamma taught me to trust in God. I just needed to remind myself of this purpose. Lillemor had never been a believer. But, unlike her, I felt that believing in God gave me a deeper appreciation of life and a higher purpose. I asked for help. I prayed for help. And I got it. I also became an avid reader of self-help books that would guide me to see who I really was, to work out what I needed to change about myself, and how to go about it.

I appreciated all the more how much of who we become as individuals stems from how we were influenced by our parents. I grew up with sarcasm and anger and shame. I think of what Dr. Larson once said about Lillemor: "Every time she looks at you, she remembers the guilt." Perhaps it was inevitable I would become sarcastic and angry and shamed, and I'm thankful I've released any tendency to those negative traits. Moreover, perhaps Dr. Larson had identified the fundamental cause of the friction that always existed between mother and daughter. My very presence was a reminder of Lillemor's forbidden love and what she had lost. I strove to comprehend what Fehlis had meant to her and the complex man that he had been.

## Chapter Twenty-Four

Who was Heinrich Fehlis? Who was my father? I had to continue my search to find out more so that I could put his life, Lillemor's, and mine in perspective.

When I look at a photograph of the youthful Fehlis, he seems like the typical well-groomed, young man from a well-to-do family. Then I look at a portrait of him in his Gestapo uniform and I don't know what to do think.

Maybe people see reflected what they want to see. Is this the face of a loving father or a cold-blooded killer? Or both? Does he look confident and self-assured, or arrogant and haughty? Authoritarian or menacing? Either way, this is the face of a ruthlessly ambitious man who did whatever was necessary to attain a high-ranking position in the Gestapo.

I couldn't sugarcoat it. This meant he bore some responsibility for the outrages committed by the Nazis. But to what degree? What specifically had he done? I felt compelled to know. I'd gone this far in my quest to unravel the mystery of my early life; I couldn't stop now.

As I mentioned, strange as it may seem, in my younger years I knew very little about the war. I didn't read any books about it, or watch any war-related movies. I lived in my own little world, my own bubble of self-protection. Apart from the occasional disclosures by Lillemor and Odd, the full horror of what had happened was not something my juvenile mind absorbed. Maybe people in Norway, in general, or my family, in particular, had good cause not to dwell on the torment of the war years. Maybe they just wanted to put it behind them and move forward. It's hard to place yourself in their shoes and imagine what it must have been like.

I do remember thinking at one point that maybe my mother, when she was with Fehlis, didn't know that he routinely sent men to their deaths. Maybe she didn't even know about the concentration camps the Nazis built elsewhere. On the other hand, maybe I was just trying to find a way to excuse her involvement with him. She worked for him at the Gestapo headquarters; she lived with him. She would have to have been blind and deaf to be unaware of the atrocities.

There was no getting away from the fact that Fehlis was a fervent member of the Gestapo under the direct control of Heinrich Himmler, one of Hitler's closest henchmen. The Gestapo brutally carried out orders that led to the Holocaust, and it rooted out and eliminated resistance fighters. The Gestapo was a law unto itself

## Chapter Twenty-Four

and acted as judge, jury, and frequently executioner. My father, whether I liked it or not, was complicit. I carried the genes of this man.

Perhaps Lillemor had been right to try and protect me from this knowledge; perhaps it was something she chose to stifle for her own self-preservation. Perhaps these were questions I had not wanted to address before. Perhaps, in some way, I was content to be kept in the dark.

### The Jigsaw Puzzle

I had to go beyond the fragments of information—sometimes inconsistent and—that my family had shared with me and conduct some formal research. I searched for other references to Fehlis in all kinds of publications, but there was surprisingly little written about a man who achieved such a prominent position, and held the power of life or death over millions.

An excellent Norwegian writer and historian, Nina Kroglund, and Berit Nøkleby, a World War II and Gestapo expert, undertook some research for me and I forced myself to read more books about the war and the Holocaust—books I'd avoided for so many years that spared no detail exposing the full horror of Hitler's Third Reich.

Kroglund, who'd written a book, *Hitler's Norwegian Helpers*, even went to Berlin and managed to get into the archives and review Fehlis's SS personnel file, which she found contained surprisingly little information. She also uncovered secret analysis of the interrogation of German POWs conducted after the war. Amazingly, one of the prisoner statements was made by Obersturmbannführer Herbert Noot, Fehlis's comrade and friend who later married Fehlis's widow, Wally.

The information I pooled from multiple sources gave me an insight into Fehlis's early career and rapid promotion through the ranks of the Gestapo. Educated as a lawyer, he was twenty-seven years old, and had just passed the bar exam, when Hitler rose to power in 1933. That same year, Fehlis joined the Nationalsozialistische Deutsche Arbeiterpartei—the Nazi Party. Within a couple of years his talent was recognized by party leaders, and he became a member of Himmler's SS and the Gestapo in Berlin. He was assigned as a government agent in May 1936.

In October 1937, he was transferred to Stuttgart and, in July 1938, he was appointed Regierungsrat (Adviser) to the government. Next, he became head of the Gestapo in Frankfurt until he was posted to Norway at the end of April 1940. His wife and one-year-old son Peter had to remain behind in Germany. In November 1940, Fehlis became chief of SIPO (Sicherheitspolizei) in Norway, the German Security Police, which included the Gestapo.

Fehlis's personnel file read: "Overall race impression: very good, Nordic; appearance: very correct and according to SS-standards. Very quiet and secure, ambitious, reliable, and good at negotiations."

Nikolaus von Falkenhorst, the German general who led the invasion of Norway and commanded the four hundred thousand troops stationed there during the occupation, described Fehlis as having "a quiet, modest nature,"

## Chapter Twenty-Four

and said he was "always very polite and tactful toward me." Of course, Fehlis was clever enough not to cross swords with the most senior military commander in the country!

During the final stages of researching and writing my memoir I came across Neal Bascomb's excellent book, *The Winter Fortress: The Epic Mission to Sabotage Hitler's Atomic Bomb*. It had a somewhat different description of Fehlis: "The thirty-six-year-old lieutenant colonel, with a lantern jaw and thin, bloodless lips, was known for his rigid efficiency and even temper . . . his subordinates only knew he was angry when the saber scar on his left cheek turned livid."

As chief of Gestapo, Fehlis reportedly ordered the torture of prisoners and he sentenced people to death, although I have not seen any evidence anywhere that he personally executed anyone. Reportedly, he had instructed that condemned prisoners be shoved into the bitter cold in bare feet and thin clothing to deter any thought of escape. He was said to have ordered most of the one hundred fifty-one executions carried out during the occupation.

As Bascomb put it, "For a man of his young age, Fehlis held extraordinary power over life and death in Norway, and he meant to use it."

## Chapter Twenty-Five

During the first years of the occupation, Fehlis worked closely with Josef Terboven, the Reichskommissar for Norway who'd seized Skaugum, the Norwegian crown prince's residence and did not hesitate to take full advantage of his position. Terboven was a petty and ruthless ruler, widely disliked, not only by the Norwegians, but also by many Germans. Even Goebbels expressed annoyance that Terboven's "bullying tactics" unnecessarily alienated the Norwegians.

Fehlis seemed to have no compunction in enforcing Terboven's hardline policy—including summary executions. Neal Bascomb outlined some of Fehlis's actions in his well-researched book. In September 1941, for instance, workers in Oslo went on strike to protest the strict rationing of milk. Their timing was bad because SS chief Reinhard Heydrich was visiting Norway. Heydrich, who

## Chapter Twenty-Five

founded the SS, and is regarded as one of the architects of the Holocaust, has been regarded by historians as the darkest figure within the Nazi regime and was described by Hitler as "the man with the iron heart."

Terboven wanted to look strong and decisive for his esteemed visitor. He declared martial law and Fehlis masterminded the arrest of hundreds of strikers and the execution of the two strike leaders.

In October 1942, Terboven declared a state of emergency in the city of Trondheim after men in British uniform, probably assisted by Norwegian resistance fighters, raided an iron-ore mine. The British RAF had bombed the SS headquarters just two weeks earlier and Fehlis's men were hungry for revenge. Ten prominent citizens were selected to serve as an example that sabotage does not pay and Fehlis's death squad shot them all in the back of the head. Fehlis then orchestrated a massive hunt for members of the Resistance, or anyone hiding contraband. The SS men ruthlessly searched homes, farmhouses, and vehicles and arrested every male Jew over the age of fifteen and ninety-one other men. Some were executed.

In November 1942, Fehlis was prominently involved in the aftermath of a famous British airborne operation that went terribly wrong. The mission was to destroy the Vemork Norsk Hydro chemical plant which produced the heavy water that was critically important for the development of an atomic bomb. An aircraft and the glider it was towing crashed and the men on board were left dead, dying or seriously wounded.

According to Bascomb, Fehlis ordered the immediate execution of four gravely injured British saboteurs; five others, still alive enough to be interrogated, were transferred to Oslo. At the Grini prison in the Norwegian capital, the five survivors were tortured for three weeks until they finally gave up the plans for the Vemork attack. Once they'd outlived their usefulness, Fehlis issued the edict for their execution. The men were driven to a forested area near Trandum, a couple of hours north, a killing field often used by the Gestapo. Blindfolded, the five were escorted into the woods, shot, and buried. Their final resting place was left unmarked.

Fehlis was merciless and efficient. The reach of his Gestapo extended the length and breadth of the country. But toward the end of the war, he is said to have adopted a softer stance and may even have ignored some extreme orders from the fanatical Terboven. I have to wonder why. Was it because he was about to become a father and dreamed of an ordinary life as a civilian once the war was over? That's what I'd like to think. Or maybe he just saw the writing on the wall, that Germany was on its way to losing the war, and he'd had enough.

**THE LEBENSBORN LEGACY**

The real bombshell I discovered through Bascomb's book was that Fehlis may well have participated in the Lebensborn ("fountain of life") breeding program, Hitler's plan to produce a "master race" of "racially pure" children, sired by SS troops. Ultimately, some eight thousand

## Chapter Twenty-Five

children, reviled as "Nazi spawn," were born to Norwegian mothers and German fathers, making Norway second only to Germany in registered Aryan births during the war.

According to Bascomb, Fehlis's Nordic appearance made him a perfect candidate. Fehlis had renounced his Catholic faith and apologized to the SS because his wife had only delivered a single child despite repeated visits to various medical professionals. Apparently, fathering just one Aryan child wasn't good enough for the Nazi hierarchy.

The implication was staggering. Fehlis may well have done his duty and had sex with numerous women. I could have more half-brothers or half-sisters. Maybe this explained the woman at the museum that Gerd had told me about, the woman who'd pointed at a photo of Fehlis and declared he was her father.

Could this be true? Was Fehlis really part of the Lebensborn program before he met and fell in love with my mother?

I guess anything is possible, but I can't for one moment believe he continued with Lebensborn once he and Lillemor were together. No one doubts the passion and sincerity of their union. But who really knows? There seemed to be no end to the revelations about the life of this complicated man—my father.

## Chapter Twenty-Six

As the tide of war turned against Germany, Terboven's personal objective was to establish in Norway a refuge where the huge army of occupation could protect the Nazi hierarchy. As a worst-case scenario, it would be the setting of the Nazi's last stand, a desperate attempt to save a remnant of Hitler's Third Reich.

Terboven was such a diehard Nazi he vowed to continue the fight, even after Hitler killed himself in his Berlin bunker on April 30. Others—Fehlis included—saw it differently. Their priority was their own survival. They had no intention of engaging in a scorched-earth battle. Fehlis, of course, was also fixated on getting Lillemor and me to safety. He knew that once the war was over, repercussions against Norwegian women who'd fraternized with German soldiers would be ugly—especially for the mistress of the despised chief of Gestapo. For her, there would be no mercy.

## Chapter Twenty-Six

As the Germans accepted the reality that they were losing the war, and it could all be over in a matter of months, if not weeks, senior German officials approached the Home Front seeking to cut deals. Reportedly, there were no end of "good" offers from Germans who wanted to save their own skins, including proposals to assassinate Terboven from people within the Reichskommissariat who had the ability and opportunity to carry it out.

Norwegian and Swedish newspaper accounts have described the "horse trade" engineered by Fehlis to smuggle Lillemor and me out of the country. Oskar Hasselknippe of *Verdens Gang* had his own inside sources because he'd been actively involved in the Norwegian resistance movement, receiving and distributing weapons, ammunition and supplies dropped by aircraft. Eventually, after the German occupiers uncovered his role, he went into hiding.

Hasselknippe, whose heroics earned him the British King's Medal for Courage, maintained that at least two members of the Norwegian Home Front were well aware of the "horse trade" between Fehlis and Söderman. In fact, it was something Fehlis had actively sought for quite a while.

Hasselknippe reported: "The demand from Fehlis for safe conduct for his mistress and baby were well known by the Home Front leadership. It was made—via intermediaries—in March, a few months before the liberation." He quoted one of the Home Front members as saying, "There seems to be nothing else that was on his mind at all." So, by this account, Fehlis could have been plotting the escape of my mother and me, even before sharing the plan with Lillemor. It sounds like he had an obsession to keep us safe, something I take as evidence that his relationship with Lillemor was meaningful and not simply a wartime affair.

The Resistance didn't get actively involved in these discussions, partly for fear that it was a trap. But the negotiations were Fehlis's private deal, something that was his highest priority even ahead of his own survival. Reichskommissar Terboven and Friedrich Rediess, the Obergruppenführer of all SS troops stationed in Norway, would not have appreciated Fehlis putting his personal affairs before that of the Reich. Söderman, on the other hand, was working with the blessings of both the Swedish and Norwegian authorities, spearheading the effort to orchestrate the peaceful handover of prisoners.

Hasselknippe observed that Söderman's "coup"—arranging the release of prisoners—earned him honor and glory after the war. It was prestige he would not have gained without the help of Fehlis. But in his autobiography, and elsewhere, Söderman never disclosed that the price of the coup was smuggling the chief of Gestapo's mistress and daughter into Sweden. That "transaction" might have taken the shine off his glory.

### Timetable to Freedom

On May 7, Hitler's successor, Admiral Dönitz, dismissed Terboven from his post as Reichskommissar and transferred his powers to armed forces commander, General Franz Böhme. At 10:00 p.m. Böhme went on

## Chapter Twenty-Six

radio and announced that the German troops in Norway would obey the orders to capitulate.

At noon the following day, Fehlis and other leading Nazis were summoned to meet with Terboven at his Skaugum residence and he read the official telegram from Donitz in which he was dismissed and the power transferred to Böhme.

### May 8, 1945

Norway was free of Nazi tyranny. In the streets of Oslo, and in towns and villages across the country, Norwegians danced all day and all night. Church bells pealed joyfully. Five years of occupation was at an end, and the celebrations were just beginning. The Allied military mission arrived in Oslo and the official surrender ceremony was arranged. As part of the surrender, the German high command had agreed to arrest and intern all German and Norwegian Nazis.

At Skaugum, according to author Bascomb, Terboven ate a sandwich and read an English detective novel. We don't know if he got to the end of the story before determining his own end. At precisely 11:00 p.m., the Reichskommissar walked into a bunker and drank half a bottle of brandy. Then he lit a five-meter fuse that led to a box holding 50kg. of dynamite. The fuse had a calculated burn of eight minutes and twenty seconds. At 11:30 p.m., an explosion rocked the estate, destroying the Reichskommissar's body alongside that of Obergruppenführer Rediess who had shot himself not long before.

Terboven had wanted Fehlis to join them in their suicide pact, but he refused. He had other plans and tried escaping with his men dressed in regular German army uniforms.

As journalist Hasselknippe wrote, "It was the best prospect for a reunion with his Norwegian family."

Going on the run was a desperate attempt to survive and possibly have a future with Lillemor and me. But that was not to be. In his final moments, with the worst having happened, did Fehlis think only of Lillemor, as he'd promised at their parting? I'm sure he did.

# Chapter Twenty-Seven

As I reflected on my life, I knew I needed to seek professional help again, so I went to a new psychiatrist. When I began to tell him how I'd discovered that my father was the chief of Gestapo, he interrupted my story, and asked if I realized he was Jewish. The thought hadn't crossed my mind and it wasn't an issue for me. It wasn't an issue for him, either. "You're lucky," he said. "I'm angry with my church."

A battery of tests performed by this psychiatrist concluded that I had PTSD—Post Traumatic Stress Disorder. I thought that was something only soldiers got when subjected to the frontline horrors of war, but it's something anyone who has been through hell experiences. My PTSD stemmed from my abnormal roots and upbringing. In a strange way, the diagnosis made me feel good. It explained a lot about my adult life and the person I'd become, and the issues I'd had with personal relationships, and especially my relationship with alcohol.

In my earliest years, all I remember being told was that my father was a general who had died in the war. I was given no specifics and I was too young to question anything. I picked up that my mother had done something wrong by being with my father, but I failed to understand what it might have been. It was only as an adult, as I began to put the pieces together like an intricate jigsaw puzzle, that I begin to see the full picture. It had taken forty years and there was still more to learn. I determined that the more I could discover about my father, the more I would be able to work out who I was. And that meant unpicking the web of lies and half-truths, the distortions and misrepresentations, that came out of Lillemor's mouth. She lied about so many things—to me and to everyone else. Maybe she even lied to herself.

When I came to know that Fehlis had been a leading member of the Gestapo, I shuddered at the thought of what that meant; what atrocities he might have committed to further the perverted cause of Hitler's Nazism.

Deciding to write the book was a struggle. Gerd, who had been so encouraging at the beginning, later questioned the value of telling the story. Would I hurt others in revealing what had transpired? Of course, I did not want to hurt anyone. I was just a daughter who, despite everything, was desperately trying to find out something good about her father. What was wrong with that? Whom would I hurt? My family in Norway? My family in Germany? Most

## Chapter Twenty-Seven

importantly, my family in America? It gave me pause, but the profound need for an historical and personal record trumped all—along with the fact that for me it was therapy of sorts.

What was good about Fehlis? Find something good, Dr. Larson had told me. There must have been something. But what can you say about a man who had a leadership position with one of the most reviled organizations in human history? My research found some inklings of the man outside of the Gestapo uniform. My father's brother, my Uncle Ingolf, had told me that he was a wonderful, generous, kind man worshipped by his siblings. My Tante Eva, who'd tried to dissuade him from the relationship with Lillemor, was struck by how handsome he was and understood why Lillemor was so much in love with him. Fehlis's SS personnel file lauded the attributes that made for a good Gestapo officer: Very correct . . . secure . . . ambitious . . . reliable . . . good at negotiations. General Nikolaus von Falkenhorst used words like polite and modest. Interestingly, both the SS file and von Falkenhorst described him as quiet.

His devotion to Lillemor and to me was obvious. As the Resistance leaders had said, he was obsessed with arranging our safe escape from Norway when the German war machine collapsed. His last words to Lillemor as he tenderly handed me into her arms were, "If the worst happens, please know that in my last minutes I will think of you and only you. Remember that, only you." Lillemor once told me he'd said earlier, "If I die, they can blame me for everything."

My heart wants to believe that this was my father: a man who was capable of deep love and devotion; a man who was willing to make the ultimate sacrifice. But I have to accept this other man: the man who had cruelly and casually tortured prisoners, the man who had ruthlessly ordered executions, the man who was villainized as the "Desk Executioner."

## My Father's Daughter

I am my father's daughter. According to what I have seen, heard, and read about him—in appearance and mannerisms, at least— I am just like him. My quest to find the nature of the man has been a long and painful journey. I don't know how I would have handled the discovery that he was the chief of Gestapo if I had discovered it earlier in my life. It was devastating enough when it was revealed to me by my German family. I have stared the specter of Fehlis in the face and survived. I used to play the "what if?" game. What if there had not been a war? What if I had grown up with two loving parents? Perhaps I would not have had problems with alcohol or made bad decisions in my own life. Perhaps I would have obtained a great education and not drank and smoked too much. Perhaps I would not have wasted years of my life.

The reality is that my father killed himself before he could be put on trial for his war crimes. The reality is that I grew up with an abusive, narcissistic, alcoholic mother, and successive stepfathers. In my earliest years, I was shunted around from one relative to the next, who all stepped in to

## Chapter Twenty-Seven

fill the void left by my mother. And to what end? At an immature age, I got pregnant and married a man I didn't love who became verbally and physically abusive. I turned to alcohol myself. I went through financial ruin. But the truth has set me free. Revisiting the episodes of my life and writing openly about what I learned has been good for the soul and maybe, just maybe, can bring some light into the lives of others facing struggles of their own.

In the end, I have accepted the burden of my parentage. In spite of what I discovered about my father I am glad that I embarked on this journey. I have accepted myself. I'm told that I have changed; that I have blossomed. I hope it's true. My great comfort is my son, my joy in life, who means the world to me. I have tried to be the loving mother that my mother never was for me.

In one of my sessions with Dr. Larson I mentioned that Mario and I had gone to see a couple of psychics. "Be careful," he warned, "They read your mind and tell you what you want to hear."

But he went on to say he'd just returned from a seminar where he'd met someone impressive. He gave me the woman's name and address and I made an appointment to see her. It was winter, the ground was covered in deep snow, and she lived at the top of a steep hill. How I managed to get up there I don't know. I was driving a little Mazda and it slid all over the place. But I was determined to find out what she could tell me. She'd said that when she was in a trance, she would speak in an Indian accent and would tape record the session so I could take it home with me.

Venke

She would not predict the future, but would focus on who I was and where I'd come from.

As the three-hour session came to an end, she said there was someone in the universe who cared for me. I'd never felt so alone and just the thought of someone caring for me was overwhelming. Such an emotional moment. Tears didn't just pour out of my eyes—they shot out. She touched my knee and said, "You are beautiful. I will give you a blessing."

> Breed and be, your destiny and vision await you.
> The beauty of your being will represent itself to you.
> Know that all that is always here for you, close
> at hand and attendant upon you.
> There is no need for you to long for anything, but know
> the truth that you are everything.
> We honor your ability to focus—to pull your directional
> energies on the highest good of all.
> And we know that when we are with you in the future,
> We will accomplish great miracles together, and you
> will look back on this day and laugh.
> And know that you have unlimited potential
> and that you have actualized it.
> And when you leave this place, you will be content
> in every aspect of your being.
> Knowing the truth.
> Feeling the truth.
> And being the truth.

## Chapter Twenty-Seven

Those last few phrases resonated with me. I had searched for the truth. I had found answers I sometimes wished I had not found. But I am the better for it. Knowing the truth ... feeling the truth ... and being the truth.

# Acknowledgments

*I* will be forever grateful to Peter and his beautiful family. They could have rejected me; instead, they welcomed me with open arms. Their loving embrace lifted my spirits and their openness gave me fresh insight into the life and character of the father I'd never known.

I also want to acknowledge Norwegian writer and historian, Nina Kroglund, author of *Hitler's Norwegian Helpers*. Nina carried out painstaking research on my behalf, took me to the war museum in Oslo, and dug through archives in Berlin to provide background on my father's wartime activities.

# About the Authors

**Venke Fehlis** was born January 30, 1945, in Oslo, Norway. Her fondest, early childhood memories were those spent in an old cabin owned by her aunt and uncle in the snowy mountains outside Oslo and visiting her grandmother's family farm in wintertime where she enjoyed horse-drawn sleigh rides.

As a twenty-year-old, Venke emigrated to New Canaan, Connecticut, where she worked as an au pair, and where she met her future husband. Eventually, they married, started a family, and built a factory in South Norwalk that manufactured steel waste containers. Afterwards, Venke launched a spa center in Greenwich, Connecticut.

In 2012, the Norwegian book (published by Historie & Kultur AS), *Gestaposjefens datter (The Chief of Gestapo's Daughter)*, chronicled Venke's life. It was a collaborative effort between her and Nina Drolsum Kroglund.

Venke is now retired and lives in a small town in southern California. When she's not at her writing desk, she enjoys playing bridge.

### Malcolm J. Nicholl

Malcolm is a former award-winning international journalist whose career included two years as Belfast bureau chief for London's *Daily Mirror*.

He has ghostwritten more than thirty books specializing in memoirs, business and entrepreneurship, how-to, health and wellness, and education, and authored seven books published in nine languages by Random House, Bantam Doubleday Dell, Ballantine Books and St. Martin's Press.

Photo: Kennedy A. Johnson

To learn more about Malcolm: https://malcolmjnicholl.com. Malcolm also runs The Balustrade Network, a full-service self-publishing company. https:/balustradenetwork.com.